WALKING
Lessons Learned in the Dark
BY FAITH

JENNIFER ROTHSCHILD

FOREWORD BY BETH MOORE

LifeWay Press®
Nashville, Tennessee

Published by LifeWay Press®
© Copyright 2003 • Jennifer Rothschild
Third printing August 2004

ISBN 0-6330-9932-5

This book is course CG-0846 in the Personal Life category of the Christian Growth Study Plan.
Dewey Decimal Classification Number: 234.2
Subject Headings: FAITH \ CHRISTIAN LIFE

Cover Design: Susan Brown
Photography: Corbis and Digital Vision

To order additional copies of this resource, write to LifeWay Church Resources
Customer Service; One LifeWay Plaza; Nashville, TN 37234-0013; fax (615) 251-5933;
phone toll free (800) 458-2772; e-mail *customerservice@lifeway.com;*
order online at *www.lifeway.com;* or visit the LifeWay Christian Store serving you.

Printed in the United States of America

Leadership and Adult Publishing
LifeWay Church Resources
One LifeWay Plaza
Nashville, TN 37234-0175

Contents

About the Authors

The phrase, "We walk by faith, not by sight" (2 Cor. 5:7, NASB) has echoed through the ages. For Jennifer Rothschild, the words are much more than a beloved Scripture; they are a reflection of how she lives.

At the age of 15, Jennifer was diagnosed with a rare, degenerative eye disease that would eventually steal her sight. It was more than a turning point for the Miami, Florida native. Her dreams of becoming a commercial artist and cartoonist faded. Words and music have replaced her canvas and palette.

Through her spiritual depth and down-to-earth style, Jennifer weaves music, illustrations, and biblical truth to help people find contentment, walk with endurance, and celebrate the ordinary. Through her story-telling and wit, they look beyond circumstances and experience God's grace in adversity.

This Bible study is based on Jennifer's trade book, *Lessons I Learned in the Dark: Steps to Walking by Faith, Not by Sight.* She also co-founded and publishes *WomensMinistry.net,* a popular online magazine. She and her husband, Philip, live in Springfield, Missouri, with their sons, Clayton and Connor. Jennifer enjoys nature walks, theme parks, and riding a bicycle built for two.

In addition to her writing and speaking ministry, Jennifer is an accomplished songwriter and recording artist, with four albums to her credit: *Out of the Darkness, Come to the Morning, Not by Sight, and Live in Concert.*

Susan A. Lanford is a writer and speaker on parenting, marriage, spiritual growth, and spiritual perspectives in healthcare. She has degrees from Texas Christian University and Southwestern Seminary. Her family is active in Second Baptist Church, Little Rock, where she teaches in the student and women's Bible study ministries and facilitates dicipleship groups. Susan and her husband, Randy, have three children, Jonathan, Jay, and Bethany, and a precious daughter-in-law, Becky.

As Susan worked with Jennifer to write the learning activities for this study, God provided wonderful prompts to her own journey of faith. She is grateful to Jennifer and praises God, the faithful One who brings light to our darkness and calls us out of darkness into His glorious light.

Foreword

When I first saw Jennifer, I knew something was wonderfully different about her. She was so young, so fresh and beautiful, yet she had a knowing in her eyes that seemed unusual for one her age.

After hearing Jennifer's testimony, I knew why her maturity exceeded her years. Her eyes revealed a knowing; and there was something indefinably chosen about her. I was seeing her similarly to how Jennifer sees—with eyes of the Spirit. I saw God's hand on her, and I've never failed to see it since.

Years ago, I attended Florence Littauer's training seminar for prospective Christian speakers and communicators. How I've laughed about receiving the brochure because I wasn't on a mailing list and had little familiarity with Florence. I'm convinced God knew I needed emergency speaking assistance! I constantly use a principle I learned there: "Do I have anything to say?" and "Does anyone need to hear it?" Beloved, Jennifer has something to say, and all of us need to hear it.

Since I met Jennifer, she has become a mother of two, a seasoned communicator, and a singer who can practically sing glory down on your head. Yet she still has the same freshness and graceful beauty that struck such a deep chord in me years ago.

Because Jennifer and her husband are great fun, I knew I was safe to make a spontaneous phone call after seeing a photo spread of their family in a Christian magazine. The message I left went something like, "OK, young lady, I'm not about to leave it to your husband to tell you how you look in that layout. Men don't tell nearly enough details. Let me just tell you that you are stunning!" I then told her how sassy and cute her hair, makeup, and outfits were. It was strictly a girl moment, but I had a feeling she'd get a kick out of it. Then I read the article. And cried. Somehow Jennifer possesses that rare, God-given combination of lightness and depth. Grace and truth. Just like the One who called her.

Jennifer's real. She knows what she's talking about. She does not have the luxury of telling and retelling a testimony of challenges long since resolved. She makes daily choices to step over seen and unseen obstacles. Jennifer is a living, breathing testimony still actively being written by the hand of God. I have a feeling this won't be the last we hear from her. I'm honored to recommend Jennifer Rothschild and her stirring new study to you. May God grant us all the gift of eyes that truly see.

Beth Moore

Introduction

I am so excited that you've joined me for this study based on my trade book, *Lessons I Learned in the Dark*. We are going to have such a great time learning what it means to walk by faith and not by sight.

We'll learn that our faith walk starts with just one step. We need to keep walking, of course, but it begins with the step of trusting God. We'll see we need to make right choices about our attitudes and responses.

Wow, I don't know about you, but I need to keep those lessons handy! God teaches us to stay in the race, following Him as we run with endurance—even when hurdles are in our path.

We may not always have God's Word at our fingertips, so we'll see how important it is to hide Scripture in our hearts so it becomes a light unto our path.

Then, we'll tackle one of the most challenging lessons of all—learning to wait on God. Isn't waiting on God one of the most difficult things we deal with?

This is not a long study, so would you commit with me to complete each day's homework during the next six weeks? Because each of our faith walks is unique, God will work through your circumstances and His Word to teach you personally.

The homework in our Bible study is simply a starting point. Listen to God and follow His direction to further study. Use simple note cards to record Scriptures that you'll be asked to remember.

Choose one person in your group to pray for and encourage. You might like to work on the Scripture memory activities together. We will have some specific things to do with our partner, but I encourage you to make this a time of fellowship and Christian growth.

And, finally, would you commit to journal during this study? Your journal may be as elaborate or as simple as you prefer. Some ladies like to make their own; some use a computer; some are happy with notebook paper. The purpose of this journal is to help you recognize growth in your faith walk, so don't wait on your facilitator or this book to tell you what to journal. Among other things, you may want to include answered prayer, needs in your life, concerns raised with your prayer partner, and the lessons God teaches you.

When we finish this study, we will not be finished walking by faith. This time together will be only a small part of our faith walk with God. I pray that each of us who begins this walk with one small step will continue so that others may see that our faith and actions work together, and our faith is made complete by what we do (Jas. 2:22).

Listening Guide

1. A Person Walking …

By _____   By _____

    Willing to take a step   Usually plays it safe

    Follows God; gives up control   Seizes control

    Responds with thankfulness   Responds with bitterness and anger

    Perseveres, endures   Quits

    Is guided by truth   Is influenced by feelings

    Is willing to wait on God   Waits on things from God

2. It can be well with your _____ even if it's not with your _____.

3. Being _____ by your circumstances is walking by _____.

4. God is your _____ when you walk by faith.

5. Lessons on the Journey of Faith

- God is _____.

- Life is _____.

- When I choose to walk by _____ and not by _____
  —no matter how hard life is—I can simply say, "It is well with my
  soul even if it may not be well with my circumstance."

Take a Step

Life's a fascinating school with countless lessons tucked in it. Some I've learned as a matter of course; others have frustrated all my attempts to comprehend. I've raised my hand time and again in life's classroom, longing for answers. I've scrutinized its textbook, yearning to understand. I've walked its hallways and climbed its stairs, searching for its meaning. Perhaps you have, too.

We learn many life lessons when times are good and circumstances easy. Others we learn in seasons of hardship, loss, and darkness. Although suffering can be the harshest headmaster, it often equips us to reach our loftiest expectations. In the adversity we dread we discover life of which we've only dreamed.

God began teaching me this lesson as a high-school sophomore in 1979. For months, I sensed my eyesight deteriorating. I was amazed at how easily classmates navigated crowded hallways—even dark stairwells. Why was I the only one bumping into schoolmates or lockers? I couldn't understand how teammates caught the softball so easily. I stood in right field, glove in hand, stared intently at the ground, and tried to see the approaching ball's shadow. Then I listened for its landing and hoped I could find it. My math grades dropped because I couldn't tell a 3 from an 8; I hadn't read my locker number for months.

Though difficult to admit, I realized this wasn't normal. I began to feel more awkward and self-conscious. At last I told my mother who immediately took me to an ophthalmologist. He eventually referred me to Bascom Palmer Eye Institute. After several days of testing, the doctors told us that I had retinitis pigmentosa, a disease that slowly eats away the retina—no cure, no way to correct damage already done. I had lost so much vision that, at 15, I was already legally blind. My retinas would continue to deteriorate until I was totally blind.

Blind … totally blind. The words sounded so final. So certain. So cold. I felt a chill inside that I'd never felt before. Nothing else was said. Silence fell on that room like shadows falling just before night. It shrouded us as we left the hospital, walked across the parking lot, got in the car, and journeyed home.

The news was probably harder for my parents than for me. My eyes were losing sight, but their hearts were being crushed. Can you imagine the heartache? How difficult it is to watch your child suffer and feel helpless to prevent it.

My dad piloted us home through the Miami streets. My source of wisdom, my counselor, comforter, and rescuer, I trusted him completely. Even though he'd also been my pastor, 20 years of ministry had not prepared him for this. I wonder if he thought, *Dear Lord, how can I fix this?* On the ride home, he was silent.

I could feel Mother's broken, tender heart and imagine her willingly trading her comfort to ease my suffering. My mom was my cheerleader, encourager, mentor, and friend. She must have wondered, *Will she be safe?* She too was silent.

Though normally strong-willed, trusting, sensitive, and talkative, that day I was silent. I remember my heart swelled with emotion and my mind raced with questions. *How will I finish high school? Will I ever go away to college? How will I know what I look like? Will I ever get a date or a boyfriend? Will I ever get married?* I remember feeling my fingertips and wondering how people ever read braille.

With almost five years of piano lessons stretched over eight, listening to me practice couldn't have been pleasant. Let's just say that I was a little short on natural talent! I did, however, practice diligently every night after dinner because if I did, I was excused from clearing the table and washing the dishes.

This time was different. Once home, I sat down at our old, stately piano with its warm, comforting sound. I began to play by ear a melody that I'd never played before. My fingers followed a pattern along the keyboard that was new to me … yet somehow familiar. I played, "It Is Well with My Soul."

Perhaps God guided my heart and hands to play that hymn. Perhaps it was a miracle that I played by ear for the first time that day, but the real miracle was that it actually *was* well with my soul. Even as I mourned my loss, I looked into my Teacher's heart, recalled His Word, and remembered His character. These allowed me to say, "Whatever my lot … it is well with my soul."

Today I still play by ear. I listen to books on tape, walk with a cane, and rely on others to drive me. I know the trappings of blindness and understand the isolation and hardships it can bring. Blindness can be painful—all life's heartaches are—but through it, God has taught me the greatest lesson in the school of suffering: Even when it is not well with our circumstances, it can be well with our souls. That was the first and greatest lesson I learned in the dark; it forms the foundation for all the lessons that have followed.

"When peace, like a river, attendeth my way, When sorrows like sea billows roll; Whatever my lot, Thou hast taught me to say, It is well, it is well with my soul."[1]

Prepare to enter the classroom:
Read Hebrews 11. Record every person's name you find in that chapter.

_____

_____

_____

_____

Day One
A Steady Pace

My friend and I stood in my new home exchanging decorating ideas. When I commented on how much I love the wallpaper in the bath, there was an awkward pause.

"But Jennifer ... how do you know you love the wallpaper if you can't see it?" It was a fair question.

I told her my mother had vividly described the Jacobean print to me, and that through her every word, I could see the honey mustard, cranberry, and forest green colors twining through the vines and leaves in my mind's eye. And I loved what I "saw" there.

That's how I like to explain faith. The dictionary says that faith is a firm belief in something for which there is no proof—a belief that does not have to rest on visible evidence. My eyes can't see my wallpaper's design, but it's still there. I know it's there; my eyes don't have to confirm what I know is real. In fact, it's so real that even though I can't see it, I still enjoy and delight in it.

Perhaps that's what the writer of Hebrews thought as he wrote, "Faith is the substance of things hoped for, the evidence of things not seen" (Heb. 11:1, NKJV).

List two things you learn about faith from reading Hebrews 11.

1. _____

2. _____

Reread Hebrews 11:1. Pause for 5 minutes (really!) to memorize this verse and meditate on its meaning.

Now, paraphrase the verse to help your non-Christian friends better understand faith:

_____

_____

With this understanding of faith, we can exercise it with the same confidence as the apostle Paul who said, "We walk by faith, not by sight" (2 Cor. 5:7, NASB).

Read in your Bible the words of Hebrews 11:13. Write the verse in your journal or on a card. Read it often to encourage you to continue to live by faith.

Walking by faith is living in a reality not yet seen. Relying on sight—as paradoxical as it sounds—blinds us to God's best. By sight, we step over God's hidden treasures that only the eyes of faith can see. Most of us never learn to walk by faith until we learn to walk in the dark. We don't lean on God until fear makes us feel shaky and weak.

List below three situations or needs in which you are walking in the dark. Circle the number that best describes any fear you are feeling (1=no fear and 10=total terror).

1. _____ 1 2 3 4 5 6 7 8 9 10

2. _____ 1 2 3 4 5 6 7 8 9 10

3. _____ 1 2 3 4 5 6 7 8 9 10

Remember this list. You'll be working more with your feelings and these situations.

When my world went dark and my fears were many, I learned that unless we trade our fear for fight, we may never find the treasures hidden in the dark. I found my future husband when I chose to risk walking in the dark. Likewise, our spiritual walk is often scary. God usually doesn't reveal what's next, and we can't begin to anticipate what the future holds.

As a loving Father, God says, "You must take a step. I've prepared you to go, and deep down you want to walk by faith." Like the faith-filled heroes of Hebrews 11, when we do step out, we find the treasures that God has reserved for those who lean completely on Him.

> When we step out in faith, we find the treasures God has reserved for those who lean completely on Him.

One way God teaches us to walk by faith is through the Bible's examples of faith that we are to follow. In fact, Paul writes, "Brethren, join in following my example, and observe those who walk according to the pattern you have in us" (Phil. 3:17, NASB).

Make your own hall of faith, listing the names of your spiritual mentors or role models. Beside each name, write a two-word phrase that describes their faith, such as *constant prayer* or *seeks God*.

_____

_____

The amazing folks we meet in the Hebrews 11 hall of faith knew how to walk by faith, not by sight ... and they learned to do so by walking in the dark. They didn't understand God's plan when they began to carry it out, and they didn't know what was coming after their first steps. Their faith became real as they exercised it—as they put one spiritual foot in front of the other. They chose to rely on something greater than sight or under-standing, and they can teach us how to walk with them on that path of faith.

Noah teaches us to go against common sense when we sense God in an uncommon way. Imagine if he had relied on sight rather than faith. Instead of building an ark, he might have opened a petting zoo!

Abraham teaches us to willingly obey even when we don't understand. If he had been relying on sight as he trudged up Mount Moriah, he might have been scanning the bushes for a lamb instead of obeying God; or he might not have started up the mountain at all.

Sarah teaches us that it's possible to believe the impossible. Surely it was not sight that prompted her to knit tiny baby blankets at her age!

Walking by faith

means taking a risk ...

taking a step ...

there's no other way.

Moses teaches us to value God's reward more than man's riches. If he had been walking by sight, he probably would have milked his position as Pharaoh's grandson for all its royal worth.

You get the idea. Faith prompted Noah, Abraham, Sarah, Moses, and the other heroes of Hebrews 11 to live the way they did. Faith prompted their seemingly peculiar behaviors which led them through God's plan ... in God's way. But walking by faith isn't easy. Each of them surely went through some internal agony along that walk of faith.

Noah experienced it, pounding one more nail into a ship in the middle of the desert. Sarah felt it with a baby's tiny kick in her once-sterile womb. Abra-ham knew it when he lifted that gleaming blade heavenward, ready to plunge it into the chest of his beloved son. (Who can imagine the agony and terror of that moment?)

Moses felt so out of his league that he begged God to send his brother Aaron to plead with Pharaoh. I can just hear him: "God, I stutter like M-M-Mel Tillis, but Aaron—he sings like M-M-Mel Tormé!"

The ground shakes beneath us when we step out in faith. But even if we feel inse-cure, walking by faith means taking a risk ... taking a step ... there's no other way.

You've just reviewed four Hebrews 11 heroes—Noah, Abraham, Sarah, and Moses. Which faith walk is most remarkable to you? Explain your answer:

_____

_____

FOR EXTRA CREDIT:
Read more about the hero you identified above:
Noah—Genesis 6:1–9:17
Abraham—Genesis 12:1-5; 15:1-21; 18:1-15; 21:1-7; 22:1-19
Sarah—Genesis 16:1-15; 17:15-21; 18:1-15
Moses—Exodus 2:1-25; 3:1–4:31

Now, answer the following questions:
Through what darkness did he or she walk?
What else do you learn about faith from his/her experience?
What do you learn about God's activity and plan for his/her life?
What application can you make in your own life from all you've just noted?

Day Two
A Confident Stride

Learning to walk on my college campus was easier knowing my mobility coach Mike was with me. If I felt wobbly, I held on to him. If I reached out or cried out, he was there. He would quickly extend his arm when I lost my footing or became disoriented. He made it possible to risk walking with a cane.

In the same way, we can hold on to God when we feel shaky in our faith walk. God Himself walks among us because we are His people (Lev. 26:12). His strong arm is always there to help us; we can reach out for Him in the dark and find Him there every time (Ps. 16:7-11). Just as Mike patiently listened to my fears, God will patiently listen to ours (Ps. 66:17-19).

Read the three Scriptures referenced in the paragraph above. Then finish this statement: "I can walk by faith with confident stride because ..."

_____

Learning to walk by faith is much like learning to walk in the dark. The mobility techniques Mike taught me gave me security in my physical stride, and they're also necessary in our faith stride. Consider the following tips for spiritual mobility.

Remain Centered

As I learned to maneuver with my cane, Mike stressed the importance of remaining centered. He showed me how to hold my cane in the center of my body. Then, with a steady arm, I would move my wrist from left to right. I did this in order to walk in a straight line and stay oriented. It allowed me to tap the sidewalk with the tip of my cane just before my next step, helping me anticipate any changes in my path.

It's essential that I remain centered to stay oriented. Likewise, we must keep God at the center of our spiritual walks. God desires always to be in the center of our lives.

"Now, O Israel, what does the LORD your God ask of you but to fear the LORD your God, to walk in all his ways, to love him, to serve the LORD your God with all your heart and with all your soul."

Deuteronomy 10:12

Respond honestly. What is the center of your life? What's most important to you?

_____

If it is not God and your relationship to Him, what must change for God and His plan to become the center of your life?

_____

It's essential to remain centered as we learn to walk by faith. Losing our center will lead us astray. "Let your eyes look directly ahead, And let your gaze be fixed straight in front of you," Solomon advises. "Watch the path of your feet, And all your ways will be established. Do not turn to the right nor to the left; Turn your foot from evil" (Prov. 4:25-27, NASB).

Being centered keeps us on our intended path. When we keep God as the center of our lives, we won't become disoriented when life casts its deep shadows. When every step is steady, we won't slip, even when the ground buckles beneath us. "My steps have held fast to Thy paths," says the psalmist. "My feet have not slipped" (Ps. 17:5, NASB).

Follow a Mental Map

I also learned it was essential to know exactly where I was going. No aimless strolling when you are blind! Mike told me to think through my path before I took the first step, to have a map locked in my mind. Knowing where I was going made every step purposeful and prevented missteps and mishaps. The map for Christians is God's Word, and when "the law of his God is in his heart; His steps do not slip" (Ps. 37:31, NASB).

When we know God's precepts, they guide us: "The steps of a good man are ordered by the LORD" (Ps. 37:23, NKJV). God's precepts also protect us. The sword of the Spirit is the Word of God, a part of the armor of light that protects us against the dark powers of the world (see Eph. 6:12,17; Rom. 13:12). This world is dark and shadowed at times. If we naively step out unprotected, we'll be susceptible to the evil influences of darkness around us. But if we wisely follow the map God has given us in His Word (no aimless wandering!), it will guide and protect us, making each step of our walk intentional. Then we too can say, "I run straight to the goal with purpose in every step" (1 Cor. 9:26, NLT).

Read Psalm 37:23; Romans 13:12; 1 Corinthians 9:26; and Ephesians 6:12,17.

Choose the Scriptures you most need to apply to the three walking-in-the-dark situations you identified in day 1. Record the reference next to each situation on page 11.

Pause to thank God for who He is and what He does in your behalf.

Listen to the Teacher

When I was learning to use my cane, Mike taught me to tune in to the music of motors. I could hear the difference between the sound of a car's engine when it was in full motion and when it was idling. Learning to recognize what was coming (and how fast) helped me know when it was safe to go and when I'd better stop and wait.

We are fortunate when we walk by faith, for we need to tune in to only one sound—the voice of our Teacher. The prophet Isaiah reminds us that we are all like sheep who wander off and need a shepherd (53:6). But to hear the voice of our Shepherd above the din of all other noises in our lives, we must be tuned in to hear His still, small voice.

Jesus said, " 'My sheep listen to my voice; I know them, and they follow me' " (John 10:27). His sheep hear and follow Him because they are familiar with His voice. When we learn to discern the Holy Spirit's voice, we'll know when to go and when to stop: "Although the Lord gives you the bread of adversity and the water of affliction, your teachers will be hidden no more; with your own eyes you will see them. Whether you turn to the right or to the left, your ears will hear a voice behind you, saying, 'This is the way; walk in it' " (Isa. 30:20-21).

When and where are you most likely to hear the Master's voice?

_____

_____

What one thing would help you hear His voice more often and with more understanding?

_____

_____

Attempt to implement this change at least once this week. You will have an opportunity to tell about your attempt during the group meeting.

Jesus said: " 'I am the light of the world. Whoever follows me will never walk in darkness, but will have the light of life.' "

John 8:12

Jesus said, " 'God is spirit, and his worshipers must worship in spirit and in truth' " (John 4:24). Walking by faith means that we allow the Holy Spirit to illuminate our eyes so that we can see beyond the here and now. Eyes of faith see every problem as solvable because they see every problem as spiritual in nature. What is merely physical is confined by the laws of nature, but what is spiritual has no confines except those our supernatural, sovereign God chooses.

As we walk by faith, the Holy Spirit helps us fix our eyes on the source of our help instead of the sting of our problems. He gently reminds us, "now we see in a mirror dimly, but then face to face" (1 Cor. 13:12, NASB). Someday the faith by which we walk will become sight. Or, as St. Augustine put it, the reward of our faith will be to see what we believe. How important it is to walk by faith! Look where it will lead us—face to face with God Himself!

Day Three
Give Your Guide a "Taste Test!"

Without a guide I can go very few places. Since the onset of my blindness, my guides have included quite a cast! I've held onto the arms of strangers in airports and the hand of my 95-year-old grandpa. I've had tall, staid men and short, squirmy boys guide me. A few women who've walked with me have said very confidently, "We're going left here," as they conspicuously turned right. (Sorry, girls, but some among us are directionally challenged!) In college, I had a guide named Karen, and more recently, one named Stephanie. Both these friends are in wheelchairs, so I hold the handles, they push … and we're off! My guides walk or roll. I trust my guides.

You know what qualifies someone to guide? Sight! Let's face it, though. Just because people can see doesn't mean they're worthy of my trust. Trust is a choice I make and a risk I take. Why? Because otherwise I'd never go anywhere! The journey is worth the risk.

My family members were my first guides. My brothers were in elementary and middle school at the time, and they learned the basic techniques right away. I loosely gripped the elbow of one and walked next to him. This meant, of course, that we had to touch. How painful for them! How agonizing for me! Cooties may be invisible, but believe me, they exist. We all had to swallow our pride.

My guide was taught to gently pull his arm behind his back when approaching narrow places to signal me to walk behind instead of beside him. It worked well. My brothers learned quickly to count steps, bark commands like "Left!" or "Right!" (they loved that part), and describe our path using a clock: "Branches at two o'clock ... duck!" They learned to guide, and I learned to trust them as guides.

It was fairly easy to trust my family to guide me. We already had established relationships, so it didn't seem too risky. I knew I could trust them; nevertheless, I still had to choose to do so.

Scripture reminds us that our Heavenly Father has grafted us into His family through our faith in Jesus Christ, and that Jesus Himself pursued a relationship with us so we could come to know and trust Him.

Circle words in the following Scriptures that help you trust your Heavenly Father.

Galatians 4:4-7

"When the time arrived that was set by God the Father, God sent his Son, born among us of a woman, born under the conditions of the law so that he might redeem those of us who have been kidnapped by the law. Thus we have been set free to experience our rightful heritage. You can tell for sure that you are now fully adopted as his own children because God sent the Spirit of his Son into our lives crying out, 'Papa! Father!' Doesn't that privilege of intimate conversation with God make it plain that you are not a slave, but a child? And if you are a child, you're also an heir, with complete access to the inheritance" (The Message).

Romans 8:14-17

"Only those people who are led by God's Spirit are his children. God's Spirit doesn't make us slaves who are afraid of him. Instead, we become his children and call him our Father. God's Spirit makes us sure that we are his children. His Spirit lets us know that together with Christ we will be given what God has promised. We will also share in the glory of Christ, because we have suffered with him" (CEV).

It's not always natural or easy to trust God. Perhaps our relationship with Him is new or untested, and we don't yet have a family photo album to flip through to remind us of His guiding presence in our lives.

That's why trust is a risk. We never learn whether someone is worthy of our trust unless we risk walking with him—and that's what God invites us to do. "Oh, taste and see that the LORD is good," David says, "blessed is the man who trusts in Him!" (Ps. 34:8, NKJV). God wants us to give Him a taste test!

In 1993, I learned about taste tests and trust as I flexed my trust muscle with a seeing eye dog! I naively assumed that I'd get a dog smarter than most humans I know, one so well trained that we'd go to the mall, I'd say, "Forward! Fifty percent off rack!" and he'd take me there! I didn't realize that I needed training as much as the dog, if not more so.

On the first day at Southeastern Guide Dog Training School, I met Jim, the trainer who tried to match each dog with just the right person.

17

My dog's name was William. If only his behavior had been as dignified as his name, but it wasn't. He was loyal, but he had a food distraction. Maybe that's why Jim paired me with William—I'm pretty distracted by food also! William was raised by people who fed him people food. So, whenever William was around people food, he wanted it so badly that he became totally distracted. Instead of focusing on me and my commands, he fixed his attention on the forbidden fodder just beyond his paws.

I realized what a serious distraction food was when William and I joined the class on a field trip to McDonald's. Proudly, the members of the class entered the restaurant one at a time with their dogs. When it was our turn, William and I stood in the doorway, and I gave him the command: "Forward." He hesitated. I'd been taught that when a guide dog hesitates, I should check in front of us for an obstruction, so I did. No table, step, or obstruction—no reason for disobedience. So I issued another command, "Forward, William," and added an arm gesture which he knew as "Move it, buddy!" Finally, he moved. Unfortunately, it was not forward. Pulling me along, he bounded into the restaurant, where he landed in a booth. With his paws on the table, he proceeded to scarf down the fries of the lady pinned in next to him.

Listening to her terrified screams, I stood in disbelief, still strapped to that food-obsessed canine. When I regained my composure, I used all my strength to pull William down from the table, commanded him to sit, cupped his ketchup-smeared muzzle in my hand, and made him look me straight in the eye. (Now remember President Clinton's affection for fast food.) So, looking in William's eyes, I said, "From this day on, I call you Bill!" and whistled "Hail to the Chief" as we marched off.

"The eyes of the Lord are toward the [uncompromisingly] righteous and His ears are open to their cry. Many evils confront the [consistently] righteous, but the Lord delivers him out of them all."

Psalm 34:15,19, AMP

Even after our shaky start, I continued to risk walking with William, and we forged a relationship. Through this relationship, I learned what makes a guide trustworthy. After more time and testing, he eventually proved to me that he had my best interests and safety at heart, and I came to trust him. It could have been different. William could have failed the test and stayed focused on those fries.

God always passes the taste test. "The Lord is good, a refuge in times of trouble. He cares for those who trust in him" (Nah. 1:7). Everything He has done through the ages reflects that; He still remains focused on us. Hmm, we read so ravenously about what God wants to do for us that we sometimes miss His expectations of us. Psalm 34:15,19 in *The Amplified Bible* describes the person God aids and rescues as one who is "consistently" and "uncompromisingly" righteous.

Our righteousness does not earn for us God's intervention, but God's intervention in our lives prompts in us a desire to live as one rightly related to Him—righteous, as one who truly trusts in Him.

What is God saying to you about your relationship to Him? Record your thoughts in your journal.

Take time to talk with God about the consistency (or lack thereof) in your faith walk.

We are all woefully inconsistent in our faith relationship to God, but never forget that—
- in the garden, He pursued us;
- in the ark, He protected us;
- in the wilderness, He provided for us;
- on the cross, He proved to us that He alone is worthy of ultimate trust.

What do Genesis 3:8-9 and Psalm 139:7-8 reveal about the way God pursues us?

_____

What do Genesis 7:11-13 and Psalm 57:1 reveal about the way God protects us?

_____

What do Exodus 16:1 and Psalm 36:9 reveal about the way God provides for us?

_____

What do Psalm 13:5; 130:7 and Romans 5:8 reveal about the way God proves that He can be trusted?

_____

Circle the word that best describes God's activity in your life right now: *pursued, protected, provided,* or *proved,* and give an example:

_____

Trust is always a response to the faithfulness of God. In your journal, write a prayer of thanks to God for this evidence of His care for you.

What is God saying to you about the way you trust in Him? Record your thoughts in your journal.

Day Four
Feelings Aren't Trustworthy Guides

Because God is trustworthy, what He says is also trustworthy. "In the beginning was the Word," says John, "and the Word was with God, and the Word was God" (John 1:1). It is impossible to separate who God is from what He says.

Read the following Scriptures. Match each one to the truth that best explains it:

1. ___ Joshua 1:5

2. ___ Psalm 119:105

3. ___ Proverbs 5:21

4. ___ Matthew 6:8

a. When life is dark, we can trust what God says, for He sees better than we can.

b. When we lose our sense of security, we need His promise that He knows what we need without our asking.

c. When God seems hidden from view, we need the assurance that He won't leave us behind.

d. Sometimes our paths are dark; at times we'll desperately need a light to guide us.

So often we don't allow God's Word to guide us. Why don't we trust God's promises in the Bible? I think it's because we trust our feelings more than we trust what God tells us.

Feelings are tough obstacles to overcome, aren't they? They seem so immediate and real. But we can learn to trust in spite of them by looking at Jesus. He knew what feelings were like—although He was fully God, He was also fully man. He came to earth clothed in humanity: "Being in very nature God, [He] did not consider equality with God something to be grasped, but made himself nothing, taking the very nature of a servant, being made in human likeness. And being found in appearance as a man, he humbled himself and became obedient to death—even death on a cross!" (Phil. 2:6-8).

We can learn to trust in spite of feelings by looking at Jesus.

Does this mean Jesus struggled with His feelings just as you and I do? Yes, it does. Emotions accompany all the events of our lives. With broken relationships come feelings of sadness or rejection. With a spouse's death come feelings of loneliness. With unjust accusations come feelings of anger. The more importance you assign to an event, the more intensely you'll feel its emotions. So when Christ approached the most important event in His life, He did so feeling an intense emotion. The Bible calls it shame. "For the joy set before Him [He] endured the cross, despising the shame, and has sat down at the right hand of the throne of God" (Heb. 12:2, NASB).

What strikes me in this passage is the word *despising*. It graphically describes how Jesus dealt with His strong emotion. This word can be translated several different ways. Different versions say Christ scorned the shame (NIV), or despised the shame (NKJV); another that He ignored the shame (AMP). In the original Greek, the word is *kataphroneo*.

Kataphroneo means *to consider with disregard* or *to esteem lowly*. What an awesome example Jesus gave us! He had feelings of shame, but He held them in low esteem.

What do you think it meant for Jesus to hold shame in low esteem?

_____

What we hold in high esteem will eventually govern us, but what we hold in low esteem, we will govern. Yes, we need to acknowledge our feelings but never to regard them more highly than God's Word. Don't ever bow to your feelings because you hold them in such high regard. Instead, make them bow to God.

We can't choose the feelings we experience, but we can choose our response to them. Our feelings don't have to dictate our choices.

Open your Bible and read 2 Corinthians 10:5. What is Paul telling us to do with our thoughts and feelings?

_____

If we esteem God's eternal Word more highly than our fleeting human feelings, we'll gain the blessings of choosing to trust. Paul tells us what happened when Jesus esteemed God's Word more than His feelings and, in obedience, went to the cross: "Therefore God exalted him to the highest place and gave him the name that is above every name, that at the name of Jesus every knee should bow, in heaven and on earth and under the earth, and every tongue confess that Jesus Christ is Lord, to the glory of God the Father" (Phil. 2:9-11).

In the first column below, list again the three situations where you are walking in the dark. (You recorded them on day 1, page 11.) In the second column, record the feelings you have had about this situation. In the third column, record a promise from God's Word that you want to esteem more highly than these feelings (you may need to review this week's material or use a Bible concordance to help in your search).

WALKING-IN-THE-DARK SITUATIONS	HOW I FEEL	GOD'S PROMISE
1.		
2.		
3.		

Recently a lady at a conference told me that even though her friend Suzy had wanted to attend, she wouldn't come with her. Suzy has the same handicap I do. "Her husband is her eyes," her friend said. "She won't go anywhere without him." Since Suzy thought her husband would feel out of place at a conference for women, she chose to stay home. Why wouldn't Suzy let her friend be her eyes for the day?

When I think about what keeps me from trusting, I realize it's fear. So why did Jesus risk everything at the cross? "For the joy set before him" (Heb. 12:2). And what was His reward? To sit down at the right hand of the throne of God. The bigger the risk, the bigger the blessing!

Who knows what blessings Suzy missed because she was afraid to trust her friend. Many of us don't realize that we, too, are afraid to trust. When we say that we trust God yet never risk acting on His Word, we really don't trust Him at all. Trust shows itself when it leaves the tip of our tongues and lands on our tennis shoes and we begin to walk—not just talk—our faith.

Yes, we all feel afraid at times. It comes in the package with our fallen human nature. But we can risk frightening discomfort to find that we really can trust God. To trust Him fully means that we believe Him and act upon what He says. When we truly believe Him, His Word illuminates our path

How would your life be different if you trusted God more and believed His Word?

_____ .

Day Five

Fear Is a Feeling; Trust Is a Choice

Fear is a natural reaction to many of life's circumstances, but trust is a supernatural choice.

The terrorist attacks on September 11, 2001, left all Americans reeling. In the aftermath, threats to airlines were a daily reality, and I struggled with the same feelings of fear as everyone else. My calendar had been booked for a year, and I was to fly every weekend after September 11. A companion scheduled to accompany me on several trips suddenly had to cancel when her husband was called to military duty. That meant that I had to make several trips alone, and I admit that I was fearful.

The atmosphere in airports and airplanes was tense, and I was not looking forward to being alone. At least a companion could help me know what was happening and what to do if there was a problem.

I remember getting on my knees before God and telling Him that I was afraid. Immediately, this verse came to my mind: "When I am afraid, I will trust in you" (Ps. 56:3).

> Trust shows itself when it leaves the tip of our tongues and lands on our tennis shoes and we begin to walk—not just talk—our faith.

God knows that sometimes fear and trust share the same heartbeat. As I meditated on the verse, I suddenly realized that "I am afraid" describes a condition, and "I will trust" describes a volition. The verse is definitive: My will can change my condition. For example, if I am down but I will get up, my choice will change my situation. So if I am afraid yet I will trust, my choice to trust God will inevitably change my feeling of fear.

When I resolved to trust God and fly, I flew without fear. Then I could quote with confidence what Paul told Timothy: "God has not given us a spirit of fear" (2 Tim. 1:7, NKJV). It's true—He hasn't. So what has He given us? The verse goes on to say that He has given us a spirit "of power and of love and of a sound mind." It is God's power in us—not our own—that gives us the ability to triumph over fear. The Bible also says that "perfect love drives out fear" (1 John 4:18); having a sound mind—taking captive every thought to make it obedient to Christ—can "demolish arguments and every pretension that sets itself up against the knowledge of God" (2 Cor. 10:5). That includes fear.

Choosing to trust God gives us the resources we need to cast out fear.

Review 2 Timothy 1:7 above. Place an X by what God has not given us, and underline what He has given us.

How are you making use of the—
power God has given you? _____

love God has given you? _____

sound mind God has given you? _____

Ironically, fear can also help us trust God. How? By making us wise. Through the years, people have talked about how much courage I must have. I must admit, I'm amused by their comments. There's a line in a popular Christian song suggesting that underneath a warrior's armor, you'll find a child. Isn't that a tender picture of someone fearlessly pursuing life, trusting our Father?

I'd like to share another picture: Underneath *this* warrior's armor, you'll find a grade-A, lily-livered chicken! It's scary walking through life in the dark.

Still, I would rather use fear wisely than foolishly waste it. So I'm learning to keep my feelings in check and exercise the kind of fear that will fuel my faith. The Bible says, "The fear of the LORD is the beginning of wisdom" (Ps. 111:10). Having a healthy reverence for God allows us to view our fears from the perspective of His mighty throne, and the wisdom that's born out of a genuine respect for Him gives us the discernment to gauge what is truly worth fearing.

Wisdom wears the garment of trust and walks without fear. Solomon said, "Wisdom is more precious than rubies, and nothing you desire can compare with her" (Prov. 8:11).

God willingly gives us wisdom just for the asking! When I was 13, I memorized James 1:5: "If any of you lacks wisdom, he should ask God, who gives generously to all without finding fault, and it will be given to him." I trust God enough to ask. So when anyone marvels at my apparent courage, I attribute it to my trusting prayer for wisdom. God has taught me to lovingly fear Him. Little else is really worth fearing.

When we fear God most, trusting Him is our wisest choice even when life is dark and scary. "Who among you fears the LORD and obeys the word of his servant? Let him who walks in the dark, who has no light, trust in the name of the LORD and rely on his God" (Isa. 50:10).

Circle names of God which have been meaningful to you this week. Remember that God's names represent His trustworthy character.

Father	Savior	Holy Spirit	Lord	Shepherd
Friend	Guide	Advocate	Provider	Love
Comforter	Creator	Bread of life	King	All Sufficient

Choose a Scripture reference from week 1—one bit of God's wisdom that is particularly meaningful to you. How can this Scripture provide the guidance you need?

Never Alone

Never alone
In my darkest hour I am never alone
Not far from home and I can feel You near me
For I am never alone

In the midst of trials there is a triumph that I know
While trusting in the One who never changes
And though my heart grows weary in the struggle of it all
I have such assurance that You hear me when I call

Never alone
In my darkest hour I am never alone
Not far from home and I can feel You near me
For I am never alone

Words and music by Jennifer Rothschild © 1990 Rothschild Music ASCAP)

[1]Horatio G. Spafford, "It Is Well with My Soul," in *The Baptist Hymnal* (Nashville: Convention Press, 1991), 410.

Listening Guide

1. God calls us to walk by faith into the darkness because He has _____ for us there.

2. Don't forfeit unseen _____ to hold onto seen _____.

3. When we journey with God, sometimes the _____ happens.

4. Faith _____, but sight _____.

5. When we allow ourselves to be dominated by _____, there is no room

   for _____.

6. Two kinds of fear exist:

   • A _____

   • Being in _____ of God

7. What we esteem _____ will govern us. What we esteem _____ we will govern.

Follow the Leader

If Webster allowed me to make one spelling change in the English language, it would be this: I would change the third "e" in independence to an "a" so that the word would read "independance." I like it so much better that way, because when the last five letters spell dance, the word makes me think of a life that is joyful and free. But then two other words would also end in dance: "dependance" and "interdependance."

See, it's all a dance ... a matter of listening to the music and learning how to respond!

Phil and I celebrated our tenth anniversary aboard a cruise ship. After our trip through the dessert line at the first midnight buffet, we realized we were going to have to do something to burn all those extra calories. So I donned sequins, and off we went to the dance floor. It didn't take us long to realize that we needed lessons, and along with several other couples, we met with the dance instructor in the ballroom.

This will be fun, I thought. Even though Phil and I had never danced before, I was determined to take the risk and not be self-conscious.

The music began, the instructor described and demonstrated each step we were to take, and Phil clumsily imitated her. I held onto him and tried to match his movements.

There we were: Phil, uncoordinated—me, blind. We stepped on each other's feet and bumped into other dancers—and we weren't doing the two-step or the bump. We were quite a spectacle!

After a while, we relaxed and began to follow the rhythm of the music. Soon we were actually dancing. It would have been less embarrassing for me and much safer for the other dancers if I'd never fox-trotted onto the scene, but oh, what I would have missed! It was worth risking my composure and revealing my clumsiness, because dancing made me feel surprisingly free.

Yes, I depended on Phil for my every move. But we knew each other so well that when we connected in the movements of the dance, it felt fabulous!

There's a lot to be said for depending on others and becoming interdependent ... a lot because, like the dance lessons, I've had to learn it all the hard way.

> "You turned my wailing
>   into dancing;
> you removed my sack-
>   cloth and clothed
>   me with joy,
> that my heart may sing to
>   you and not be silent.
> O LORD my God, I will give
>   you thanks forever."
> —Psalm 30:11–12

Textbook Treasures:

" 'If anyone would come after me, he must deny himself and take up his cross daily and follow me. For whoever wants to save his life will lose it, but whoever loses his life for me will save it' " (Luke 9:23–24).

"Whatever was to my profit I now consider loss for the sake of Christ. What is more, I consider everything a loss compared to the surpassing greatness of knowing Christ Jesus my Lord, for whose sake I have lost all things. ... I want to know Christ and the power of his resurrection and the fellowship of sharing in his sufferings, becoming like him in his death, and so, somehow, to attain to the resurrection from the dead" (Phil. 3:7-11).

Prepare to Enter the Classroom:

A wonderful week is before us. The Colossians verses we will read confirm an amazing truth: God is unambiguously for us—in Jesus Christ!

Read Colossians 1:3-14,21-23; 2:6-8; 3:1-17; and 4:2-6 and record on a card each phrase that describes your life in Christ. Allow these words to remind you of Jesus Himself present with you and for you. Place these cards in your home, office, and car. Spending this week reminded of your life in Christ will set your mind and heart in the best attitude to receive our lessons for this week.

Choose from this week's study a verse to memorize that will help you with right attitudes. Practice saying it with your accountability partner.

Day One

Celebrating Dependence Day

Like other 18-year-olds, I saw going away to college as a major step to independence. As a freshman at Palm Beach Atlantic College, my greatest desire was to blend in. I didn't want to be known as "the new blind girl." I just wanted to be known as the new girl, so I loved that often it wasn't obvious that I couldn't see. It was as if I could hide my blindness behind a facade that made me feel normal.

Near the end of orientation I felt educated, irritated, placated ... and dilapidated! Worn out, I decided to spend some time alone in the chapel before the final meeting.

The college campus is located on the intracoastal waterway, and the chapel was in the waterside amphitheater. To get to it, I had to cross a busy four-lane thoroughfare. By that time, I was accustomed to listening for traffic. I stood confidently on the edge of the curb, ready to cross. But I didn't extend my cane because I didn't want the drivers of the passing cars to know I was blind.

So I waited until I heard a lull in the traffic, took a deep breath ... and ran! One lane, two lanes ... whew!

The cars in the third and fourth lanes were going the opposite way. Terrified, I couldn't tell what was coming from where. I almost ran into a car, and the driver slowed just long enough to yell some choice locker-room words. I was humiliated, but I made it safely across.

I staggered into the amphitheater and collapsed into a seat. My adrenaline rush faded, and I began to think about what I'd done. *I'll never do that again, God, I promise!* And I meant it! That close call squelched my desire to look normal and be independent.

Sitting there alone, I realized independence is not all it's cracked up to be and it often isolates. The same is true when we act independently of God. The children of Israel learned a similar, yet far more painful lesson.

Exodus provides an account of these lessons. What happened in—

Exodus 16:1-4: _____   Exodus 19:1:_____

Exodus 19:20: _____   Exodus 31:18:_____

The nation was dependent on God for their deliverance from Egypt and their pilgrimage to Canaan. Yet they acted independently of Him while Moses was on Mt. Sinai.

Exodus 32:1-6 tells about their independent action. Why did the Israelites act independently of Jehovah?

_____

What was the consequence of their insulting, independent act?

_____

What were the consequences of a time when you acted independently of God?

_____

Fortunately, an unintended consequence of our self-reliance is to reveal our need for a helper—a Savior.

Back at Chapel by the Lake, after I repented and regrouped, I realized I had no way to get back. My meeting was in 20 minutes! Hoping a student would walk by, I decided to stay put. I prayed as I listened for pedestrians.

Five minutes passed. Silence. Ten minutes. Silence. Far from blending in, I was totally alone, and I imagined college staffers out looking for the new blind girl.

A deep voice interrupted my thoughts: "Miss, do you need help?" I spun around. It was a police officer.

"Well … actually …," I stammered. Then, swallowing my pride, I told him all about my misadventure. When I finished, he was really excited.

Excited? He was scheduled to work security for chapel service. He'd been watching a football game when he felt an urgency to leave for work—more than an hour early. He told me, "I am a Christian. I knew God was nudging me to go." Now he knew why.

I was stunned. A stubborn, self-absorbed girl sat by the water and prayed. A kind and merciful Father answered. An obedient and loving policeman came to help.

Though I don't know that officer's name, I do know his Heavenly Father's name. It's *Jehovah-Jireh,* the God on whom I depend.

Jehovah-Jireh:

the God on whom I depend

Let's head back to Mt. Sinai and those confused Israelites in Exodus 33:2. Notice God's provision in spite of their stubbornness and self-absorption. What two things did God do for them?

_____

What a merciful God who provides for us even when we isolate ourselves from Him.

God knows our needs. He knew about the needs of the Israelites, and He knows your needs too. Furthermore, Philippians 4:19 states clearly that He alone can supply our needs. Sometimes, though, instead of depending on God, we seek to meet our needs in our own way. Bad idea! Have you ever seen the catchy phrase: "Man plans; God laughs"? What a difference when we seek God's plans for meeting our needs.

Read Jeremiah 29:11-13 and James 4:13-15 in your Bible. Now, pause to thank God that you are in a state of dependence on Him, His riches, and His plans for you!

Day Two
Risking What You Can't Lose

One of many reasons we can depend on the Lord is that His name bears His character. Most of us are only mildly acquainted with His name—we know about Him and of Him. But God is intimately acquainted with us—He knows us.

What evidence that God intimately knows you do you find in Psalm 139:1-4?

_____

_____

_____

One of our basic needs is to be known. Yet human companionship cannot provide the intimate knowing that our soul craves. God alone can offer that because He knows us completely. When I accepted this wonderful truth, I could admit that my desire to be known by Him is greater than my desire to be independent.

Sometimes I have isolated myself by choosing to be independent, but more often I have felt isolated because independence has chosen me. Here's what I mean. Sometimes I feel that blindness is a burden not to be shared.

Part of the isolation results naturally from the fact that blindness is a mystery comprehensible on a cognitive level but baffling on an intuitive level. I find that pragmatists tend to casually dismiss it, while the tenderhearted enter into it with a degree of sympathy that prohibits real connection. Some even romanticize it, marveling at how perceptive I must be or how acute my other senses are.

Many things create islands of people's lives. We all find ourselves in situations where we feel isolated from others because we think they cannot truly understand our circumstances. As a result, a feeling of loneliness descends—soul-loneliness.

It makes me cry out to be connected to someone who understands without words or explanation.

What produces soul-loneliness in you? _____

_____

Examine the connection between your soul-loneliness and the walking-in-the-dark situations you identified last week (p. 11). Explain:

_____

_____

Circle on a scale of 1-10 whether you are more or less dependent on God because of your soul-loneliness (1=totally independent and 10=totally dependent).

1   2   3   4   5   6   7   8   9   10

Unsought independence—soul-loneliness—can teach us to depend on the One who knows us intimately. It makes us want to know God even as we are known by Him; it also helps us to risk allowing others to know us—becoming interdependent. That's the life God designed for us. God knows us fully and makes us eternally secure in Him. When we put our precious independence in His hands, we risk something we can't lose.

During college orientation, I learned that dependence isn't really so bad. Later in my freshman year, I learned that we are richer if we risk being interdependent.

I called mom with two important pieces of news. "Mom," I announced excitedly, "I went out with this guy named Curtis. And he wears an earring!" I heard a gulp and then a faint sigh. "And I drove Allison's car this morning!"

"You ... what!" Mom's voice was no longer faint.

"It's true, Mom! We all piled in the car and went to the bank's empty parking lot. It was so much fun!"

I wish I could remember mom's exact words because I'll probably need them with my kids when they do something foolish! I distinctly remember that she was not happy! The good news was that dating the guy with an earring now seemed completely harmless.

Our relationship with God inevitably affects our relationships with others, and they will find us fully reliable only when we depend fully on Him.

Well, I never did either again, but I learned a lesson from driving Allison's car. It was just another step in my dance lessons: Dependence is a good thing ... and interdependence is even better! I was totally dependent on Allison to tell me when to turn, when to brake, and how fast to go. But Allison also had to depend on me to do what she said. Life is like that little car crammed with college students. In order to navigate the turns and deal with the bumps in the road, we must rely on the driver's handbook—God's Word. We're all on the journey together, and our lives are filled with people who need us to be dependable. Our relationship with God inevitably affects our relationships with others, and they will find us fully reliable only when we depend fully on Him and His Word.

Look up the following verses and list how we are to interact with one another.

John 13:34 _____   Ephesians 4:32 _____

Romans 12:10 _____   Ephesians 5:21 _____

Romans 12:16 _____   Colossians 3:16 _____

Romans 14:13 _____   I Thessalonians 5:11 _____

Romans 15:7 _____   Hebrews 10:24 _____

Galatians 5:13 _____   James 4:11 _____

Ephesians 4:2 _____   I Peter 4:9 _____

Can others count on you to put into practice the above "one anothers"? Place a check mark beside the three "one anothers" that are the most difficult for you to apply.

Philippians 2:13 says, "It is God who works in you to will and to act according to his good purpose." Pause and ask Him to work in you to fulfill His purposes in your "one another" relationships.

When we fully depend on God, we're ready to dance.

We will be fully reliable only when we follow the precepts of His Word and depend fully on Him. I'll never forget hearing an old country preacher explain the meaning of fellowship. Instead of a Greek word, I heard, "It's two fellers in a ship!" Well, in a way, it is. We are all on this journey of faith together. God is the captain of our souls, the precious Father from Whom all the family derives its name.

We all have times when we aren't completely reliable. When we don't depend on God for direction, we can fail others and ourselves. But when we've traded our independence for the freedom of fully depending on God and the fullness of depending on each other, we're ready to dance. We just have to listen for the music!

Day Three
Listening for the Music

In 1996 we moved to Oklahoma. We had been there a few weeks when the local TV station was aflutter with warnings: the first tornado of the season was on its way. Our only TV was downstairs, so I trudged down the stairs, pillow and blanket in hand. I was going to watch the weather till the storm passed. By the time I settled on the couch, the winds were howling, and the windows were rattling with every gust. Just as predicted, hail and lightning accompanied the wind, and the rain came in monsoon-like swells. It was enough to scare even this Florida girl!

As I cowered beneath the blanket, I noticed between wind gusts and thunder crashes the chirping of what sounded like newly-hatched baby birds. The sweet sounds were entertaining at first, but they quickly became annoying when Mama bird joined the chorus. Mama was a full-throated whistler—and oh, was she loud! The soundtrack that evening was a dissonant mix of hail, thunder, wind, chirping, and whistling. Those birds never quit. Between swells, the storm grew silent, but not once did those birds stop singing. Why aren't they scared? Don't they know there's a storm? This is not the time to sing!

When the storm died down and I began to feel sleepy, it dawned on me. Those birds knew there was a storm, but they sang because they were birds. They responded to the life that was inside them, not the storm that was outside them.

Sometimes storms surround us, and the discordant sounds of our circumstances are so loud that they drown out the music. But deep inside us is a song that can rise from God's presence in our life. Even when the storm rages, our response can echo the melody of freedom within us.

So how can you dance when your independence has left you feeling lonely and isolated? How can you dance when you feel stuck in dependence? How can you dance when interdependence fails you and you find yourself in painful circumstances?

We can all take dance lessons from Peter at this point. You remember Peter ... Jesus referred to him as the rock. Not really the name of a dancer, but I think the old fisherman can teach us the dance of faith.

Take a moment to read about His dance lesson in Matthew 14:22-33.

Peter and the other disciples found themselves in the midst of a stormy sea. The wind tossed their boat and tested their courage. Suddenly, they saw someone walking on the water. Jesus identified Himself, and Peter found his partner for this storm-tossed dance.

What did Peter request in Matthew 14:28? _____

What did Jesus reply (v. 29)? _____

Jesus invites us to dance, too. No matter what storm rages, He beckons each of us, as He did Peter, to come toward Him, risk trusting Him, and find Him fully faithful.

You know the story. Peter stepped out of that boat into a perilous place that revealed his absolute need for God. Once there, he realized how hard it really is to dance ... especially over the waves.

What happened when Peter saw the raging wind (v. 30)? _____

The Bible tells us that when he saw the raging wind, he became afraid and began to sink. Peter saw the storm raging because he took his eyes off the Lord of the dance. And when he did, the din of the chaos surrounding him drowned out the sound of the Lord's music of freedom. Peter was failing dance lessons at this point. As he was sinking from the weight of his faithlessness, he cried out three words—the same words that will keep all of us in step with the rhythm of grace.

Read Matthew 14:30, and record the three key words Peter spoke.

_____

Verse 31 records Jesus' immediate response to Peter's cry. What did Jesus do and say?

_____

Sometimes our utter dependence makes us stumble awkwardly toward the arms of God. Sometimes we totter precariously as we learn to strike just the right balance in our inter-dependent relationships. God knows we are weak and wobbly dancers. He is always ready to extend His arm and catch us.

" 'Lord, save me!' " are my three favorite words in the book of Matthew. I spoke them as a frightened college student stranded at Chapel by the Lake. I whisper them quietly to my Heavenly Father today as a wife and mother learning to walk by faith. They are the three most powerful words any of us can speak when we're learning how to dance, for they invite the Lord of the dance to teach us the steps of freedom that come from full dependence on Him.

Don't wait for the storm to pass before you sing. Don't wait for just the right situation in life before you let your spirit loose to dance. You can dance in the dark or when the storm rages. Lean fully on the Lord. Listen closely, and you'll hear His music in your spirit. Rely on Him for your every step, and you'll experience the joy and freedom of dependence.

Unfailing Love

I will trust in Your unfailing love
My heart rejoices in Your salvation
I will sing unto the Lord
For He has been good to me

Your goodness like the rainfall
Washes over me
I dance beneath the starlight
As You're dancing over me
Joy is now my heartbeat
Freedom is my song
So I soar on the wings of Your love

I will trust in Your unfailing love
My heart rejoices in Your salvation
I will sing unto the Lord
For He has been good to me

Words and music by Jennifer Rothschild © 1997 Rothschild Music

Day Four
Charting a Course Through Thorns

Biblical scholars speculate Paul's thorn could have been a difficulty such as epilepsy or failing eyesight, or even his persecutors.

How does Paul describe his difficulty (2 Cor. 12:7)?

_____

Perhaps Paul's weakness is described in general terms because we don't need to know the specific struggle to understand what it means to have a thorn. I guess that's because we all have them. Maybe your thorns are what you listed in week 1 as your walking-in-the-dark situations. A thorn is anything that makes us feel we are not in control of our lives. They are a part of our fallen world. Unfortunately, we often don't deal with them effectively.

Sometimes we mismanage the weaknesses in our lives. When we do, we can look a lot like these girls.

Matchless Martyr displays her thorn proudly for the benefit of all those "who have no idea what true suffering really is." She uses her thorn to create feelings of guilt and punish those whose lives are too easy. She lifts up her thorn to God as her humble sacrifice, reminding Him and everybody else of her elite status in the kingdom.

Perfect Pollyanna disguises her thorn's scars. She plasters on a smile and hides her suffering behind religious rhetoric. Regardless of the pain her thorn might be causing, she emits a series of bouncy platitudes like "Praise the Lord!" and "Isn't God good?"

Determined Denier has the lumpiest rug in town because she constantly shoves her thorn under it—as if disowning it will make it go away. She's not blaming or sugarcoating; she's denying it exists.

Do you recognize in the examples above your strategies for coping with your walking-in-the-dark situations from week 1? Explain your answer:

_____

Paul shows us a better way to deal with our thorns. He didn't deny his thorn or the problems it caused.

Underline in the margin Paul's prayer regarding his thorn. Have you ever asked God for something similar?

_____

"Three times I pleaded with the Lord to take [my thorn] away from me."

2 Corinthians 12:8

35

The depth of his struggle and the pathos of his prayer imply that it affected him deeply.

I can understand that prayer. I've prayed that way before, and you probably have, too. Our thorns produce pain and suffering, and like Paul, we need to lift them to God in prayer. Also like Paul, we can be content with God's answer.

What did Paul receive according to 2 Corinthians 12:9?

_____

God gave Paul something better than removing the thorn. Paul received the grace to deal with his weakness so God's strength would be clearly seen.

Sometimes God delivers us *through* the thorns instead of *from* them. Why? So His grace can grow there and His strength can sustain us there. And so we can learn how to travel in tandem with Him. Remember, Paul's thorn was God's showcase, and a thorn is never a platform for spotlighting ourselves.

- If I used my blindness as a badge of martyrdom, I would glorify myself ... as a Matchless Martyr.
- If I sugarcoated the suffering associated with my sight loss, I would confuse people and distort the true message of God's grace. God is good, and He is worthy of my praise, but unlike Perfect Pollyanna, my thorn hurts at times. When it does, it's OK to cry ... and I do.
- Shoving my thorn under a rug would only trip me up. If I deny the frailty associated with my blindness, I miss the strength of God that can be released in my weakness. The Determined Denier never experiences such a powerful moment.

Only after I admit my insufficiency, yield it to God, and receive His grace do I have something about which to boast.

FOR EXTRA CREDIT
Read 1 Corinthians 1:26-31.
1. Describe God's strategy.
2. Why does God use this strategy?
3. How does this strategy redeem our human tendency to boast?

Remember that you know and are known by the sovereign God who is in control of every part of His creation. He sees when a sparrow falls. He knows the thorns that bring you pain. God is able to use evil people and evil acts to accomplish His glory and our good. God used Pharaoh to provide deliverance for His chosen people; He used Caesar Augustus to give Joseph and Mary a reason to be in Bethlehem at the appointed time; He used Pontius Pilate to send His Son to a cross to bring redemption to the world. God is in control of Satan and his actions; Satan can never act outside the limits God sets. So give Him your thorn. If He doesn't remove it, find your sufficiency in His grace alone.

You know and are known by the sovereign God.

We sang "I Surrender All" almost every Sunday when I was a child. Our church used it as an invitation to come to Christ. Perhaps you could sing those words to Christ today as an invitation for Him to come to you—providing His strength as you yield your weakness.

Day Five
Abiding by Passenger Protocol

One of the frustrations Phil and I experienced early in our married life was our inability to enjoy recreational activities together, so one day Phil came home with the remedy—a bicycle built for two. On my second night of traveling tandem, I traded in my desire for control for the joy of following—but only by learning some passenger protocol. But I'm getting ahead of myself; let's take a look at what I learned.

1. Loosen your grip

On my first tandem bike ride, I gripped the handles so tightly that my knuckles turned white. In a frenzied, futile attempt to stay in control, I held in a death grip the only thing I felt I could control. Don't we all do this?

I also did this with our closet; let's just say Phil never understood the concept of hangers. His side looked like a group of men had been there when the rapture occurred … piles of shirts, belts, shoes, and pants—all left behind! I was convinced this was something I could control. I thought if his shirts were hung according to sleeve length, my world would seem orderly. Let's face it: I was trying to control him, not his closet!

That kind of control is a myth. My behavior created the *illusion* of control, and Phil became pretty disillusioned with me because of my controlling behavior. In the end, I still felt the insecurity of being out of control, and he felt the shackles of being overly controlled. I've since learned to grip the doorknob more loosely when I open the closet.

Did you know that an unreasonable desire for control is a form of greed? Jesus had a lot to say about greed. He told of a rich man with such abundance that he didn't have enough room to store it, so he tore down his old barns and built new ones.

What parallels do you find between your life and the man's life in Luke 12:13-21?

_____

_____

My pastor once explained that a better translation of verse 20 would be: "They will require your soul of you," with *they* referring to the barns, fields, and wealth that had become his god.

This Luke 12 man fell for the illusion that he was in control of his world and that his future was secure. He's known as the rich fool because, unfortunately, he died that night and could not enjoy his bounty. Quoting my pastor again, "If we bury our hearts in the perishable, then we will perish with it."

Greed, however, isn't reserved only for material things. If we hold anything in a death grip, it's a form of greed. It may make you feel as though you're in control, but it leads to death. A control freak never enjoys life—and people who share closets with control freaks don't enjoy life either! On the bicycle built for two,

Holding things in a death grip is a form of greed.

I was holding those handle bars in a death grip, and my knuckles turned white because it cut off the blood supply to my fingers.

We all need to be reminded not to choke the life out of things that aren't really important. Jesus said, " 'Do not worry about your life, what you will eat or drink; or about your body, what you will wear. Is not life more important than food, and the body more important than clothes?' " (Matt. 6:25). So hold things loosely and learn to rest.

What is God telling you about needing to loosen your grip?

On which situations? _____

On which people? _____

On which concerns? _____

Use the words of Matthew 6:25 to compose a prayer that expresses your needs regarding control of your life.

_____

_____

2. Rest where you are

Paul's example of how to live with thorns suggests that we rest in our weaknesses. If we settle into the position His grace has placed us, we'll see His strength made perfect there. And we'll experience the joy of our journey following Him.

Instead of resting, though, many of us resist where God places us. We heap guilt on others who don't seem to have it as bad or perhaps subject others to a litany of complaints.

Such behavior is a red flag signaling that we're resisting. Part of learning to follow is flying the white flag of surrender. We surrender to the position in which God has placed us, and we surrender our behavior in that position.

When you stop to think about it, it takes incredible effort to gripe and micromanage. What an energy drain! Instead of creating burdens for ourselves by our negative behavior, we can unburden ourselves as we submit all to God and simply rest. Jesus said, " 'My yoke is easy and my burden is light' " (Matt. 11:30). If you feel that the weight of your circumstances is too heavy to bear, maybe it's because the burden is yours, not His.

On one flight, I sat next to a young woman who was flying for the first time. I marveled at how calm she was. After some small talk, I finally asked: "Why aren't you nervous? Most people are scared, or at least uneasy, on their first flight."

"Well, I'm not a pilot," she said. "Even if something happened, I couldn't do anything about it. So I might as well relax." Her answer struck me as very profound and a great example of what it really means to rest.

Many of us go through life resisting our circumstances because we operate under the mistaken notion that we are in charge. I once saw a bumper sticker that said, "God is my co-pilot." That sounds spiritual, but it isn't true. The truth is that on our faith journey, God is the pilot, and we follow. We aren't invited into the cockpit because we are not in charge of the journey. Our pilot is completely trustworthy. We need not fret, for He is capable of navigating through any turbulence. So we can rest wherever He has lovingly placed us. And when we do, we'll experience the fabulous freedom of following.

Once I learned to relax from the backseat of the bike, riding in tandem was a pleasure. I had relaxed and could enjoy the journey from my place on the bike.

What is God telling you about your need to rest where you are?

In which situations? _____

With which people?_____

Regarding which concerns?_____

Use Matthew 11:30 to compose a prayer that expresses your needs regarding trusting God where you are. Write your prayer in your journal.

3. Follow the one in front

As a rookie tandem bike rider, I learned rather quickly that only one of us could be in front. I found that awfully frustrating because I love being in charge.

For years, my desire for complete control masqueraded as the socially acceptable trait of perfectionism. I was a meticulous housekeeper, burning the midnight oil to make sure that even nonessentials such as baseboards and blinds were immaculate. Much to the torment of my family and friends, I insisted that everything in my home match perfectly. And when it came to my clothes, the standard was beyond perfection. I was a prototypical, type-A, firstborn perfectionist!

Living by faith means

God leads, we follow.

I'm still a firstborn, but I'm recovering from my perfectionism because it's really hard to be a blind perfectionist. Blindness has crucified the perfectionist in me, one hammer blow at a time. To follow God, we must die to our own desires, one hammer blow at a time.

"I have been crucified with Christ," Paul writes, "and I no longer live, but Christ lives in me. The life I live in the body, I live by faith in the Son of God, who loved me and gave himself for me" (Gal. 2:20). The desire for complete control denies us the power available to live a crucified life. God is the one in front; living by faith means that God leads as we follow.

My problem on the backseat of a tandem bike wasn't my lack of control; it was my unwillingness to yield my desire for control. On our journey of faith, we struggle with the same tension. It's hard to let go of our desire to be in charge, but the life of faith requires us to trust the Lord completely and not our own clever convictions.

Proverbs 3:5-6 describes this choice well. Read these familiar verses. What other words could you use in verse 5 for "understanding" (NIV; KJV), "judgment" (CEV), or "insight" (AMP)?

_____

_____

Learning to release control and willingly follow is essential for traveling the path God has chosen for us.

The tandem bicycle's second seat is a place of submission; in a spiritual sense, it reminds me to yield control to the One who is trustworthy, capable, and knows exactly where I need to go. He alone can get me there the best possible way. How silly for any of us shortsighted sinners to bark commands at the One who sees all of eternity.

Since God Himself goes before us and prepares the way, following His loving leadership is the surest, safest way to travel.

Listening Guide

1. Walking by faith demands that we give up _Control_ and _follow_ .

2. Walking by faith gives us the opportunity to _restfully_ _follow_ .

3. Compensating for Our "Thorns"

   • The Matchless _martyr_

   • The Perfect _pollyanna_

   • The Determined _denier_

4. Removing your "thorn" will not be _sufficient_ ;

   only _GRACE_ is sufficient to meet your need.

5. Sometimes following God means you have to deal with _thorns_ .

   Sometimes He doesn't deliver you _from (out of)_ the fiery furnace, but

   far more mercifully, He chooses to deliver you _through_ that furnace.

Choose the Right Response

We had just moved into our new home in Springfield. Things were barely out of boxes—and I was almost out of my mind—no big surprise! Since the 1960s, researchers have put moving near the top of the list of significant stressors. But it's especially stressful if you're blind.

Having an orderly world makes life workable for blind persons. Everything has a place, and everything's in its place. Moving, then, is the antithesis of order. Chaos reigns—nothing has a place, and even if it did, it wouldn't be in it!

So on moving day, I have to unpack all the boxes, touch each item, and literally put it in its place. When I'm finished, my kids can use me as their own personal tracking device. Why waste your energy searching the house for something when Mama's brain is equipped with GPS?

Phil had helped me mark all the appliances with raised dots and tactile markings, and the kitchen was serviceable, so we graduated from delivered pizza to homemade lasagna. I preheated the oven, prepared the lasagna, and opened the oven. First attempt … ouch! Second attempt … ouch! Third attempt … a very loud and unladylike ouch! I fought that lasagna into the oven, and I have the battle scars to prove it!

As I nursed my wounds, I longed for my orderly world again. My stinging arms were painful reminders of how difficult change can be. I didn't like tripping over boxes and feeling my way around our new domain. "I'm tired of making adjustments, Lord," I cried. "I'm tired of personally unpacking each box so I'll know where everything is. And I'm tired of bumps, bruises, and burns!"

No one heard me except God. Whew! I was already beginning to hear that violin playing dirges for my pity party, one where no one would have wanted to join me.

Sometimes it's good to let it all out … and I did. God is a patient listener. But there's a fine line between inviting God into our heartache and gearing up to send invitations for the "poor me" event of the year. In fact, nowhere does God sanction pity parties! Instead, the Bible says: "Consider it pure joy, my brothers, whenever you face trials of many kinds" (Jas. 1:2). If we think of a trial as joy, our response will be to rejoice. I read that and think, Learning to rejoice when our world heats up and life stings—now that's tough!

James doesn't say *if* hardships come; he says *when* they come—and they will come! That's reality—which means we'll certainly have opportunities to rejoice! Throughout the New Testament, we are told to rejoice in our trials.

That got me to thinking about what joy really is. One Old Testament Hebrew word translated as our English word *joy* means *a special goodness in the widest sense*. When I realized that's what God intended this trial of moving to be for me, I no longer wanted to whine. I wanted to rejoice! Now there's a reason to strike up the band and throw a party!

Textbook Treasures:

"Rejoice in the Lord always. I will say it again: Rejoice!" (Phil. 4:4).

" 'In this world you will have trouble. But take heart! I have overcome the world' " (John 16:33).

"Weeping may endure for a night, But joy comes in the morning" (Ps. 30:5, NKJV).

Prepare to Enter the Classroom:

Read the book of Philippians—the epistle of joy! This response toward God and toward a life of joy is essential for our subject this week—choosing the right response. Record phrases or truths about joy and rejoicing that you find. Choose one or more verses to memorize.

_____

_____

Day One
See Through Grateful Eyes

Do you remember the robot in the TV show "Lost in Space"? Most of his screen time consisted of his waving arms, flashing lights, and intoning warning: "Danger! Danger!" I often feel like that—like my blindness sends out a silent signal saying: "Warning! Danger!"

Most women can say to a friend, "Let's go shopping!" If I make the same suggestion, I fear my friend really hears, "Will you pick me up, lead me around the store, pick out clothes, read labels, and be my mirror? Will you place my pen so I can sign for my purchase, drive me home, and walk me into the house?" Whew! That's more like a complicated, full-time job than a simple friendship!

Sometimes reality is hard, but I believe I've learned that our perspective on adversity can exert more power than the hardship itself. If beauty is in the eye of the beholder, so are pain and heartache. Even though blindness has been a difficult gift to receive, I now accept it with thanks. As I've learned to view my circumstances from God's perspective, I've also learned to receive gratefully. I've learned that what at first looks like a complication can actually be an extraordinary blessing in disguise.

Look Through the Ordinary

I once took a creative writing class. "I want everyone to stare at this chalkboard and imagine it's a window," the professor announced. "Then write about what you see."

One student gave mind-numbing details of a football game he was watching from his luxurious skybox. Another more imaginative soul saw delicate snowflakes and ice-capped mountains. Yet another saw the cemetery that beckoned him toward his father's grave.

Keep in mind—we really saw an ordinary chalkboard. What we see through life's windows depends on our souls' perspectives. God may see extraordinary potential in the things we see as just ordinary.

Read Moses' amazing conversation with God in Exodus 4:1-17. What ordinary things did God use to equip Moses for his extraordinary tasks (vv. 2,6,9,11,14)?

_____

_____

What extraordinary thing did God do with Moses'—

staff? (See Ex. 14:16; 17:5-6.) _____

hand? (See Ex. 9:22; 10:21.)_____

Describe how God might use these ordinary things for His glory.

Telephone _____

Kitchen_____

Vehicle _____

Money_____

Pencil_____

Look at the Bigger World

Shifting our gaze can help. When blindness frustrates and discourages me, I think of a man named Tony who is a gifted singer and plays the guitar masterfully with his feet. He was born without arms. He can drive a car, read a book, and see his surroundings, but he can't embrace his wife or hold his children. When I think about that, I genuinely thank God for what I have, because it's so much greater than what I've lost. Sometimes it's difficult to see others' bigger problems because what we're dealing with seems so big.

Read Matthew 6:25-34. What did Jesus teach about perspective on our daily concerns?

_____

_____

Paraphrase verse 34 so that it speaks to a specific worry or concern you have today.

_____

_____

I didn't say to dismiss our heartaches as trivial because someone else has it worse. Someone will always have it worse, and we will always have heartache. I simply suggest that shifting our gaze to a bigger problem has two advantages: (1) It puts our own situations in perspective, and (2) It prompts a grateful attitude that releases us from bitterness.

Read in Acts 10:1-28 the Apostle Paul's tutorial for seeing the bigger world. Cornelius' world was Roman, pagan, and military. Peter's world was Jewish, strictly religious, and newly Christian. How did God make both of their worlds bigger?

_____

_____

Notice that Gentile, God-fearing Cornelius prayed regularly. Recall that Jewish Christian Peter was praying when God spoke to him and that he was known as a praying man (see Acts 3:1; 9:40). Praying people see the bigger world and God's activity in it!

What was Cornelius enabled to see? _____

What was Peter enabled to see?_____

Look Toward the Heavens

Shifting our gaze heavenward, we focus on God and His promises. When we choose to view life from that lofty perspective, our grateful eyes will see God's goodness all around us.

One of those promises is in Psalm 84:11. Write its promises here.

_____

Jesus' promise to "the pure in heart"—those single-mindedly focused on the things of God—is that they will see God Himself. Job 19:25-26, Psalm 17:15, Isaiah 6:1, 1 Corinthians 13:12, and 1 John 3:2 all share this theme. Take time to read each one. Record in your journal the reference and key words that are meaningful to you.

How does this perspective—looking toward God, even seeking God—speak to you and any difficult gift you are receiving?

_____

_____

Day Two
Discover the God of Grace and Glory

I know you've been diligent and given your Bible a workout. So today, we're going to rest in God's presence and discover what His glory looks like. Get a cup of coffee and your cordless phone. You'll see why.

Before I lost my sight, my career goal was to be a commercial artist. I loved to draw! I had several years of lessons, and cartooning and lettering were my forte. I inherited my talent from my mother, who is quite the artist.

Mom had a special knack for training her children to perceive every color in the spectrum. It was rare for her to use less than five adjectives to describe a color. I knew what red looked like when it was warm and orangey on a tomato's skin. I knew how to see the beautiful blue undertones beneath a fire engine's red paint. I loved the color yellow, whether splashed on an ear of corn or lying gently on a buttercup. Even though my eyes no longer see color, every one I ever saw is still fresh and vibrant in my mind's eye. There I can still see all the hues of colors I ever saw.

How special, then, when Clayton came home from preschool and showed his grandmother's eye for color. By age three, Clayton had learned that for his mommy to see, he needed to use words. So he held a crumpled paper toward me and said, "Mommy, look at this beautiful flower," and began describing his beautiful picture. "Mommy," he said, "the flower is pink. And the leaves are not just green, they are a yellowish green."

I remember sitting on our front porch, holding his picture in my hand. It could have stabbed me as a painful reminder that I would never draw again, never have the opportunity to enjoy art with my son. Instead, I felt amazed that Clayton's little eyes could perceive the difference between a bluish and a yellowish green.

It was as if God had illustrated a beautiful picture of His goodness. It was as if I could see a shade of His grace I'd never seen before. I wouldn't have seen that beautiful grace if God had not already taught me to see through grateful eyes.

Grateful eyes see God's glory as well as His grace.

Grateful eyes see God's glory as well as His grace, and God's glory is what turns the pictures in our lives into beautiful works of art. Mentally thumbing through the album of my life, I see many snapshots that at first glance don't seem very delightful. But when I look closer, through grateful eyes, I see them bathed in God's radiant glory.

For example, one spring evening I arrived in Florida to speak at a women's conference. I didn't feel well at bedtime and assumed I just needed a good night's sleep, but I awoke in severe pain. In the local emergency room, I quickly learned what kidney stones are.

Surgery took the place of my speaking engagement. I was very discouraged. Had I flown across the country just to be stuck in a hospital? It was hard to be grateful for such a strange turn of events, but Peter's words ran through my mind: "Dear friends, do not be surprised at the painful trial you are suffering, as though something strange were happening to you. But rejoice that you participate in the sufferings of Christ, so that you may be overjoyed when his glory is revealed" (1 Pet. 4:12-13). It was the verse I would have spoken on the night before, and it encouraged me to go ahead and rejoice. So I did. I chose to be grateful in what God had allowed. I knew from Matthew 24:27 that Jesus would someday burst like lightning through the eastern sky, and I'd see His glory. And then, I thought, I'll be more than joyful—I'll be overjoyed.

What I didn't expect was His glory to burst into my hospital room. I heard a soft knock and the door opening. "Jennifer," a female voice said, "you don't know me, but I work here. I saw your name on my computer screen. You spoke several years ago at a conference I attended when I was battling breast cancer. God used you to help me, and I had to come to say thank you. By the way, my name is Gloria."

Gloria! Just like that, God's glory! God shone a spotlight on that strange, painful incident in my life and turned it into a beautiful picture for the album of my life. I didn't have to wait for "someday" to see His glory revealed; His glory had walked into my hospital room. Gloria's words of encouragement allowed me to see God's goodness and to blot out my discouragement. I was overjoyed by how God used my difficult circumstance.

How do you rejoice over God's use of difficult circumstances?

_____

_____

_____

Call another member of your study group, read what you've written, and discuss your thoughts together. End your call by praying for each other.

I'm convinced God often wraps difficult gifts in His grace—and then uses them to display His glory. We are the ones who truly benefit when we choose to gratefully receive them.

Day Three
A Life of No Wasted Moments

We assume that gratitude would be easy if God would only remove our difficulties, that feelings of gratitude would then well up, overflowing in praise to God. Right? Believe me, the chances of that happening are slim. According to Luke 17, I have to conclude they're just 1 in 10.

Read Luke 17:11-19, Jesus' encounter with 10 lepers. Then record the facts of this story as if you were a reporter trying to write a page-1 story.

Who? _____

What? _____

When? _____

Where? _____

Why? _____

Your story's headline: _____

Jesus was on His way to Jerusalem when ten lepers called out to Him to have pity on them. Their disease-ravaged bodies made them outcasts in a society that considered them unclean. So they cried out for Jesus to show them mercy, and He did. One immediately came back to find Jesus, "threw himself at Jesus' feet and thanked him" (v. 16).

Where were the other nine? Why didn't sheer gratitude catapult them back to Jesus? I wonder … until I look in the mirror and realize that I scurry through my busy life like those nine. You see, when I was eight years old, I received an unmerited gift: the redemption of my soul through the mercy in the rugged wrappings of the cross. It has given me light in the darkness, water in the desert, and hope amid sorrow.

Yet I, too, forget to say thank you. Like the heedless and healed nine, I hurry on my way, savoring the gift but forgetting all about the Giver.

May we all be like the one, rather than the nine. May we all be like the leper who exhibited his faith by choosing to give thanks.

Why didn't sheer gratitude catapult the nine lepers back to Jesus?

Does your response toward life's difficulties better match with the nine lepers or with the one who returned to thank Jesus? Offer an explanation for your answer.

_____

_____

I once thought of faith as a recipe for getting what I wanted from God. If that were true, it would mean that if I could muster enough faith, I would no longer be blind. But faith is not meant to offer an escape from life's difficulties; its purpose is to give us strength in the midst of them. God allows hardship because of His great mercy and love for us, and He often removes it for the same reason. However, we should not thank Him more fervently on the day our difficult gift is removed than we do on the days we carry it. It takes just as much faith to bear a burden as it does to believe that it can be removed.

Your faith shows itself in a attitude of thankfulness in all circumstances. Bitterness never kneels at God's throne; it just shakes an angry fist. Gratitude, like the lone leper, throws itself before Christ. When you smash the last brick of your wall of bitterness with the hammer of gratitude, you will hear the echo of the words Jesus spoke to the leper: " 'Your faith has made you well' " (Luke 17:19).

Have you come back, thrown yourself at His feet, and thanked Him for the difficulties you're experiencing today? Until you do, you'll never experience the healing that your faith can provide.

In the space below write a prayer thanking God for the lessons He is teaching you through your difficulties.

> **We should not thank God more fervently on the day our difficult gift is removed than we do on the days we carry it.**

_____

_____.

If you are not yet willing to thank God for these lessons, talk to your patient God and Savior about why you hesitate.

Remembering God's great gift of salvation makes all other gifts pale in comparison. All of us who have received it need to come back to Jesus and throw ourselves before Him, praising and thanking Him loudly. When we learn to be truly grateful for His greatest gift, we'll learn to gratefully receive any other gift He may allow.

"You are worthy, our Lord and God,
    to receive glory and honor and power,
  for you created all things,
      and by your will they were created and have their being" (Rev. 4:11).

FOR EXTRA CREDIT

Strengthening our discipline of prayer is key to our being thankful in all circumstances. Read Matthew 6:9-13 and Luke 11:2-4 Jesus reminded His followers to include these key elements each time we pray:

1. Acknowledge God's holiness.
2. Submit to and commit to God's purposes.
3. Ask God to meet your physical needs.
4. Ask God to forgive you and commit to being forgiving in His hearing.
5. Recognize the power of evil.
6. Celebrate God's power to overcome evil.

These elements are personalized every time you pray. Take time to do that now:

My Father, You have shown me Fatherly love through _____

and that I need to be reverent and respectful of You through _____.

You have revealed Your holiness to me by _____
and how I thank You.

Thank You for accepting me into Your family (date/place) _____

and giving me a place of service in Your kingdom as I _____.

I need Your will to be done in_____,
and I commit myself to doing what You reveal Your will to be.

My basic needs today are _____,
and I trust You to meet them. I will not waste my energy worrying about them.

I have forgiven _____ and want to forgive _____
who has wronged me.

I ask You now to forgive me for _____.

Today, I'm tempted to _____.

Satan's power is strong to lure me toward these things. Father, I trust Your much stronger power to lead me away from temptation. I commit myself to follow Your leadership and trust in You, Your love, mercy, grace, and care. Amen.[1]

Day Four
Delight in the Discipline That Strengthens

When we rejoice in hardship, we acknowledge that God permits it for a purpose—to discipline us. I've got to tell you: *discipline* is not my favorite word! In the past I have misunderstood it. Parenting, however, has taught me that the true nature of discipline is training, not punishment.

That's God's use of discipline, too—not to punish us, but to change us. He allows suffering to be like the hurdles we must jump to strengthen us.

My friend Katharyn willingly subjects herself to the torture of running marathons. I don't know why. Personally, I enjoy running my mouth, running the dishwasher, and running to the mall. But running 26.2 miles? Yikes! Katharyn disciplines herself and trains hard to succeed in a marathon. Months in advance she wakes before sunrise and starts to run. As the days progress, her route lengthens. Even though it's never easy, her training pays off. By the time of the marathon, she is lean, strong, and ready to race.

You should see her at the end of the race! She looks like someone ran her skinny body through the washing machine, bleached the color out of it, and then wrung it out relentlessly. Katharyn doesn't care what she looks like when she crosses the finish line. Her goal is to finish, and it's worth training and running those punishing miles just to do so.

> **The true nature of discipline is training, not punishment.**

Spiritual training and discipline enable us to finish our spiritual race. Paul said, "I buffet my body" (1 Cor. 9:27, ASV). His verb could easily be mistaken for *buffet*—you know, like the midnight smorgasbord on a Caribbean cruise! But no one runs marathons on such a buffet. In the original Greek, the word *buffet* actually means *to discipline by hardships*. A runner will discipline himself and endure arduous training in order to be fit for the race. It's not easy ... but it is effective.

In your life, what buffets you—trains you for your race of faith?

_____

Reflect and truthfully answer: Have these buffetings strengthened you for your race or prompted you to sit out of the race? Explain your answer.

_____

_____

Even though discipline is intended to produce deep-seated character change, it can cause us pain. "God disciplines us for our good, that we may share in his holiness. No discipline seems pleasant at the time, but painful. Later on, however, it produces a harvest of righteousness and peace for those who have been trained by it" (Heb. 12:10-11).

Using Hebrews 12:10-11, list in the left column below each benefit you accrue from God's discipline. In the middle column, place a symbol to indicate your response. In the right column, identify one area of your life where you need this benefit from God.

⊘ Not detected in my faith or my life		
🎁 Glad for the gift, but unwilling to endure hardship to open it		
✝ Drawn closer to Christ through this		
💡 Just realizing this benefit has come to me through hardship		

Benefits of discipline   My response   I need this benefit ...

shared holiness   🎁   with relationships.

_____   _____

_____   _____

_____   _____

God allows suffering to discipline us; our choice is whether to discipline ourselves to respond with rejoicing. Both forms of discipline will strengthen us. I'm not convinced that suffering alone creates strength. It's our response to suffering that does that. The discipline of rejoicing in suffering is a response that bears fruit. We can rejoice even in suffering because of the harvest of peace and righteousness we will certainly enjoy when the training is complete.

The Book of James reminds us of the result of rejoicing in suffering: "You know that these troubles test your faith, and this will give you patience" (Jas. 1:3, NCV). We all need a good dose of patience—now! Interestingly, the original Greek word means more than passive endurance. It refers to the perseverance that actively overcomes the trials of life.

A great example of this kind of patience was the brilliant composer Ludwig van Beethoven. When he realized that he would be deaf—a musician's greatest nightmare—he said, "I will take life by the throat." That's the kind of tenacity James is talking about.

What additional truths about patience do you learn from these Scriptures?

Proverbs 19:11 _____

Romans 12:12 _____

1 Corinthians 13:4 _____

Galatians 5:22 _____

Ephesians 4:2 _____

Colossians 1:11 _____

Colossians 3:12 _____

1 Thessalonians 5:14 _____

Perseverance results when we rejoice in suffering. Look at God's promise: "We also rejoice in our sufferings, because we know that suffering produces perseverance; perseverance, character; and character, hope. And hope does not disappoint us, because God has poured out his love into our hearts by the Holy Spirit, whom he has given us" (Rom. 5:3-5).

God's loving purpose is to conform us to the image of His Son, and Peter reminds us that persevering in trials is how we become more like Him.

Carefully read 1 Peter 1:3-9,17-21 and note every truth you learn about Jesus.

_____

_____

Verse 8 reminds us that we love Christ even though we have not seen Him. Read similar thoughts expressed in John 20:29 and 1 John 4:20. How is your faith strengthened or weakened because you do not see Christ physically?

_____

_____

Notice the words in 1 Peter 1:21: "your faith and hope are in God." The character produced by rejoicing in hardship is Christlike character—His glory revealed in us— and that character produces hope. Fill in the blanks from Romans 5:3-4.

_____ produces _____

_____ produces _____

_____ produces _____

> "Hope does not disap-
>
> point us, because
>
> God has poured out
>
> his love into our hearts
>
> by the Holy Spirit."
>
> **Romans 5:5**

Romans 5:5 tells us we experience three things in the midst of and at the end of our difficulties: (1) a hope that does not disappoint us, (2) God's love poured out into us, and (3) God's Holy Spirit with us! No wonder we can confidently expect God to use our painful circumstances for good. These three gifts turn our hardships into a special goodness in the widest sense. Hope is not a wishful "What if?" but is certain and confident that "He who has begun a good work in you will complete it" (Phil. 1:6, NKJV). Hear our Savior's words just before His own undeserved suffering: " 'In this world you will have trouble. But take heart! I have overcome the world' " (John 16:33).

Day Five

Joy Comes in the Mourning— and in the Morning

When Clayton was eight months old, he fell headfirst onto the sidewalk out of his stroller. We were very concerned about a possible concussion, but he seemed fine. Over the next three days, however, he grew increasingly uncomfortable and fussy. Eventually he became listless. We were in and out of doctors' offices and hospital emergency rooms. He didn't have the symptoms of a concussion, so doctors were baffled. I didn't know medicine, but I knew my son—and I knew something was dreadfully wrong.

When Clayton began vomiting, we took him to the doctor again. There was so much blood in Clayton's diaper that he was whisked away to surgery. Clayton's large intestine was turning itself inside out. The severe damage took several hours to repair.

Friends quickly arrived to give blood and offer prayers. We were on our knees in that waiting room asking God to help our baby when our surgeon interrupted our prayers with the news that the operation had been successful. "I know you have prayed to your God," he told us, "because your baby should not have survived. It's a miracle that he didn't have to have a colostomy." We knelt in humble adoration of our Great Physician.

Home alone that night, I thought about how close we came to losing Clayton. To drown out the silence and calm the emotions churning inside me, I sat at the piano and began to play. As I did, a song began to form in my heart and move beneath my fingers:

I will rejoice in You
God of my salvation
You always see me through
And I will rejoice in You!

All that remains of that dark July day in 1990 is a physical scar. Over the years, as Clayton has grown larger, his scar has become smaller. When he got old enough to ask me about it, I told him that it meant "God takes care of us."

Perhaps you too have a scar. You may have trouble rejoicing in it, but think of your scar as a showcase of God's power to take care of you and you will rejoice in the Savior who strengthens you. When you do, God will use your joy to minister to others.

A Mourning that Ministers

My friend Joni had been married five years when her husband learned that he had cancer. This was neither what she had envisioned at the altar when she and Vance exchanged marriage vows nor what she had anticipated when their baby girl was born two years later. Vance and Joni prayed through all his treatments and hospitalizations and believed in God's healing, even when a hospital bed replaced their living room furniture.

One afternoon, Joni left Vance's bedside to answer the phone. When she returned, she realized that her prayers and belief for healing had been answered. God had lovingly and ultimately healed Vance by gently ushering him into heaven.

I met Joni shortly after Vance died, early in her mourning process. There were some days when taking a shower was her paramount achievement, and on some days her sentences began with a laugh and ended with tears. There were days when she couldn't find any words at all.

The way Joni mourned was a ministry. Her sorrow was a showcase for the joy of the Lord, which became her strength. I watched her walk boldly through her heartbreak with the kind of perseverance we've studied this week. The joy of the Lord strengthened her even on the darkest days—and it was contagious.

I remember shopping with Joni a couple of years after Vance died. It was near Memorial Day, and she wanted to buy flowers for his grave. We began to look through the flower arrangements at our local supercenter.

"These all look awful," she said. Then, systematically, she picked up each arrangement, "This one's ugly …This one's wilted …This one's turning brown." Finally, in frustration, she set the last flowers down and said, "These are so ugly, if I put them on Vance's grave, he'd just die!" We giggled awkwardly—and then roared with laughter!

> Choose to rejoice in spite of difficulty — suffering strengthens faith, joy showcases God's power, and mourning ministers to others.

Often it's hard to rejoice in our circumstances. The difficulty of change, the sickness of a loved one, the pain of loss—these seem to give us little reason for rejoicing. But if you choose to rejoice anyway, your suffering will strengthen your faith walk, your joy will showcase the power of God, and your mourning will minister to others. You have God's word that "He will give beauty for ashes, joy instead of mourning, praise instead of despair" (Isa. 61:3, NLT). So if life presents you with a burn, a scar, or wilted grave flowers … rejoice! "Rejoice in the Lord always. I will say it again: Rejoice!" (Phil. 4:4).

Rejoice in You

I will rejoice in You
God of my salvation
You always see me through
I will rejoice in You

Out of the darkness, into the light
Healed from blindness, given new sight
Walking in victory, power, and might
I am triumphant over the fight

A song of deliverance now I can sing
Your love has conquered; death has no sting
New every morning mercies you bring
I shout it boldly, You are the King!

Adapted from words and music by Jennifer Rothschild
© 1993 Rothschild Music (ASCAP)

Circle the phrases in the song above that are most meaningful to you. Using your Bible concordance, look up verses that use the key words you circled. Jot down in your journal references and key thoughts in the Scriptures you find.

Each day this week we studied one of five principles to choosing the right response.

1. See Through Grateful Eyes

2. Discover the God of Grace and Glory

3. A Life of No Wasted Moments

4. Delight in the Discipline

5. Joy Comes in the Mourning

Place a plus (+) beside the principle where you sense the greatest peace and a check mark (V) beside the step you feel God is asking you to take in your journey of faith.

---

[1]Adapted from "Life Helps: Discipline of Prayer," *Disciple's Study Bible* (Nashville: Holman Bible Publishers, 1988), 1761.

Listening Guide

1. Sometimes _____ _____ come into your life.

2. To walk by faith and not by sight, we must learn to _____ our

_____ to the circumstances.

3. Part of God's Will

- _____ always.

- _____ without ceasing.

- We are in everything to give _____.

4. God does not _____ heartache, but He _____ it sometimes.

Run with Endurance

For several summers when I was a teenager, I attended a Christian camp in Black Mountain, North Carolina. One summer early in my blindness, I arrived at camp without my cane. It hadn't yet become an extension of my right arm, and I was still at a point where I didn't want it to be obvious that I couldn't see. I preferred muddling through without my cane, going only to places with which I was familiar.

One night a group of girls decided to wrap the car of the cutest guy in camp, and I was not going to miss the fun. We were thrilled with the success of our covert operation until we heard the sound of a car coming toward us. "It's camp security!" someone cried.

We immediately began to run. As we fled, I instinctively grabbed a fellow escapee's arm. In our frenzied flight I lost my grip, lost the group, and lost my footing. I did, however, find a tree. *Smack!*

I ended up in a ditch, totally disoriented and pretty sore. One of the girls quickly returned to help me, and we ran for home.

We are to "run with endurance the race that is set before us" (Heb. 12:1, NASB). Believe me, I learned the hard way that we can never run with endurance when we're running where we're not supposed to be. If I'd resisted the temptation of that forbidden flirtation, I would have been safe in camp.

Sometimes we *are* in the right place, running the race God has marked out for us, trying to run with endurance. So why do we sometimes stumble, lose our way, feel we're about to hit the wall?

It's because often unanticipated hurdles are in our path. We can clear these away only by stripping away anything that could weigh us down or trip us up as we run. That's why in the same verse we are told to "lay aside every encumbrance, and the sin which so easily entangles us" (NASB). This is what you and I must do as we start this week's awesome topic.

> "I guide you in the way
> of wisdom
> and lead you along
> straight paths.
> When you walk, your steps
> will not be hampered;
> when you run, you will
> not stumble."
> —Proverbs 4:11-12

Textbook Treasures:

"Watch out that you do not lose what you have worked for, but that you may be rewarded fully. Anyone who runs ahead and does not continue in the teaching of Christ does not have God; whoever continues in the teaching has both the Father and the Son" (2 John 8-9).

"Do you not know that in a race all the runners run, but only one gets the prize? Run in such a way as to get the prize. Everyone who competes in the games goes into strict training. They do it to get a crown that will not last; but we do it to get a crown that will last forever. Therefore I do not run like a man running aimlessly" (1 Cor. 9:24-26).

Prepare to Enter the Classroom:

This week's preparation will be radically different. May God bless you for your courage as you begin. Your assignment is simple, but it is not easy: Confess your sins—

- that entangle your time;
- that entangle your relationships;
- that entangle your Christian discipline;
- that entangle your physical health;
- that entangle the life priorities to which you claim to be committed.

Read Isaiah 53, asking God to make clear the cost of your sins. Record in your journal what you sense God saying to you through His Word.

Finally, read Psalm 51, asking God to restore life to you as He did to David after he confessed.

Day One

Throw Aside Every Weight

A guide dog can be a good thing, but I finally accepted that William wasn't helping me with the life I needed to live. One day he bolted onto the platform at my church while I was singing. Once at the mall, he relieved his bladder right in front of my favorite store. What a mess!

Many incidents like these had made me feel like giving up with a guide dog; it all came to a head one Sunday morning when he chased a grasshopper that was loose in my Bible study room. I was so embarrassed by the disruption that I excused myself to hide in the ladies' room. My friend Lori was right behind me, and I burst into tears. "It's just not working," I cried. "This is more of a liability than an asset. I've never wanted to quit so badly before, but—I don't know if I should."

Lori responded judiciously. "Jennifer, if you were deaf, you'd want to wear hearing aids that fit your ears. It would be discreet and practical. I don't think you'd function as well with big ol' Mickey Mouse ears hanging on either side of your head." I giggled with relief at Lori's homespun Southern wisdom. "Giving the guide dog back doesn't mean you're giving up or giving in just because it's hard," she said.

William could get me safely where I wanted to go, but for me, he wasn't the best thing. Instead of enhancing my busy life, he hindered it. Any good thing can weigh us down if we substitute it for what is really best.

Read Jesus' parable of the sower in Luke 8:4-15. Notice that some hear the Word of God and begin to desire Him. But what soon happens according to verse 14?

_____

One pastor commented on these verses: " 'The pleasures of this life' and 'the desires for other things'—these are not evil in themselves. These are not vices. These are gifts of God. They are your basic meat and potatoes and coffee and gardening and reading and decorating and traveling and investing and TV-watching and Internet-surfing and shopping and exercising and collecting and talking. And all of them can become deadly substitutes for God." He summarized by saying: "The greatest adversary of love to God is not his enemies but his gifts."[1]

> " 'I know the plans I have for you,' declares the LORD, 'plans to prosper you and not to harm you, plans to give you hope and a future. Then you will call upon me and come and pray to me, and I will listen to you. You will seek me and find me when you seek me with all your heart.' "
>
> **Jeremiah 29:11-13**

Ponder those conclusions. Ask God if you are weighed down by His good gifts so that you do not seek or desire Him, the Giver. Pray about what you sense is true in your life.

Endurance isn't a virtue if you persevere just to prove you're not a quitter. The point of running with endurance is to run well and finish the race—to do God's will as we follow the course to the finish line. Once in a while we must assess our lives: is there anything we need to shed? Think about it. Serious runners don't carry ice chests, extra clothes, and a fast-food meal. These are all good things, but they don't help runners during a race.

The Bible uses this race imagery to explain the need for endurance and staying the course with Christ. Read again the textbook treasures (p. 59). Circle the words or phrases from those Scriptures that you most need to improve your running. Choose one to memorize this week. Write it on a note card to begin your memorization.

In order to run well, we must listen to God. He has great plans for us and knows the best way for us to succeed.

One of the most beloved Scriptures on this topic is Jeremiah 29:11-13. Read it now.

Describe the wise response to God's plans stated in verses 12-13.

_____

What is the wonderful promise God makes to you in the first part of verse 13?

_____

What is the one condition that makes the promise fulfilled in your life (v. 13)?

_____

Read Deuteronomy 4:29 and Matthew 22:37-40 in your Bible. What are the best words to describe your love for God? Choose any from the list or add your own.

Estranged	Passionate	Faint	Convenient
Satisfying	Attached	Impersonal	Discordant
Ardor	Affectionate	Liking	Detached
Dispassionate	Exciting	Enthusiastic	Earnest
Genuine	Bothersome	Lukewarm	Committed Fondness

Based on the words you chose, what will you do this week to deepen your love for God?

_____

What one action will you take to purify your love for God, (for example, become more single-mindedly devoted to Him)?

_____

Day Two
Run to God

Like the rich young ruler, we also run to Jesus with needs only He can meet. Jesus looks at us with His penetrating gaze and loves us with His enveloping love, but then His plans for us seem like too great a sacrifice and not what we want to hear.

Whatever that sacrifice might be, it's small compared to the prize we receive in Jesus' presence. So don't run to Him with preconceived notions or an agenda. Run to Him just to be with Him. Run to Him with abandon. Fall before Him, and cling to Him alone.

Read about the rich young ruler in Mark 10:17-22. What need did he perceive in his life?

_____

How did Jesus feel toward the young man (v. 21)?

_____

Did Jesus' reply to him in verse 21 demonstrate that He loved him? Explain below.

_____

_____

How do you account for the ruler's sadness as he left Jesus' presence (v. 22)?

_____

_____

Jesus knows what you need, and you'll never be disappointed by His provision. In fact, you will be amazed and overwhelmed, just like the folks in Mark 9:15: "As soon as all the people saw Jesus, they were overwhelmed with wonder and ran to greet him." They saw something the rich man missed—someone who was worth everything. If you truly see Him, you too will be overwhelmed with wonder, and you will run to Him.

> "Patient endurance is what you need now, so you will continue to do God's will. Then you will receive all that he has promised."
>
> **Hebrews 10:36, NLT**

When was the last time you caught a glimpse of Jesus? What were you hearing, seeing, sensing, feeling, deciding? Offer any details you can remember.

_____

_____

_____

Remember that after you've run a while, the race begins to feel long. You pound the pavement, winded and weary, and can easily get discouraged or feel like dropping out before the finish. Charles Spurgeon felt that way often; he tried to resign 32 times! Like him, we need the reminder of Hebrews 10:36. Staying in the race requires something more substantial than not quitting or wishing our needs were met. It takes something more gratifying than yearning for the goal. It takes a deep desire for God. David often expressed his desire for God.

The following phrases are from various translations of Psalm 63:8. Underline the one that best describes your relationship to God:

"My soul clings to you" (NIV).

"I follow close behind you" (NLT).

"I stay close to you" (CEV).

"I hold on to you for dear life" (The Message).

"My soul follows close behind You" (NKJV).

"My whole being follows hard after You and clings closely to You" (AMP).

Notice how this verse concludes: When our souls follow hard after Him, He holds us up with His strong right hand.

Do you remember running laps in physical-education class? I do! I remember panting after a hard run. Using an analogy, the psalmist David said: "As the deer pants for the water brooks, So pants my soul for You, O God" (Ps. 42:1, NKJV).

What analogy describes your desire for God and its effect on you?

_____

I want to know what it feels like for my soul to pant after God with the psalmist's kind of intensity. When we run to Him with that strong desire, we'll be breathless, and He becomes the air we breathe.

I was eight years old when I ran to Jesus the first time, for my salvation. Now the path to Him is familiar and well-worn. I run to Him daily because I desire to know Him. And though I don't deserve it, God Himself runs to meet me, too.

Perhaps you remember a vivid scene from the 1992 Barcelona Olympics which poignantly illustrates this. A young British runner was prepared for the run of his life. Derek Redmond's lifelong dream was winning a gold medal in the 400-meter run. The gun sounded in his semifinal heat, and Derek was running well until a pulled hamstring sent him sprawling facedown on the track.

Determined to finish the race, Derek somehow got to his feet and began to hop toward the finish line. An older man made his way down out of the stands. Showing the same determination as the injured runner, he pushed aside security guards to reach Derek. The spectators watched Jim Redmond throw his arms around his son Derek, supporting him until they crossed the finish line together. The onlookers were on their feet, weeping and cheering.

Derek Redmond didn't win the gold medal, but he knew his father loved him too much to stay in the stands, watching him suffer. That's the kind of Heavenly Father we have ... a Father who loves us too much to stay out of reach when we struggle and suffer.

Jesus told a story of a father with two sons to explain God's response to us when we come to Him.

Read this beloved parable in Luke 15:11-32. Now, describe—

the older son: _____

the younger son: _____

the father: _____

Luke 15 has been called the chapter of lost things. What was the loss of—

the older son? _____

the younger son? _____

the father? _____

In the midst of loss, how do you explain the father's desire to celebrate his son's return?

_____

_____

When your race seems too long and you begin to lose heart, remember:
1. Your Heavenly Father runs to meet you as you struggle to run to Him (Jas. 4:8).
2. You do not run alone, nor are you blazing some untested trail (Heb. 12:1).
3. You may become tired on God's running plan, but you are never disqualified from the race. You may not be the flashiest runner, but He promises you will always be upright and your feet will be sure (Prov. 4:11-12; Isa. 40:29-31).

Day Three
Our Pride and Our Falls

At the end of one semester, I began packing and watching for my father to come and move me home. Dad arrived to mounds of neatly-packed stuff and issued orders on which items to take and in what order. We must have made 30 treks up and down those stairs. Finally, only hanging clothes were left. With them, I took charge. I told Dad which clothes to take first and how to carry them. I saved the best for last—my nicest suits and dresses—certain I was the only one who could carry them correctly and put them in just the right place. I folded the generous stack over my arm and headed down the stairs.

"Wait, I'll come get those," Dad called out. "Oh no, Dad, I'm fine," I replied. Confidently, I continued speeding downward.

"Be careful You're going too fast," he called again. "Really, Dad. I'm fine." I pranced down the stairs with my treasures—in charge, in a hurry, and invincible. Only three steps from the bottom, I began to tumble. All I could think about were my beloved clothes! Instead of dropping them so I would have a soft landing, I held them high to protect them!

Mentally and physically unbalanced, I collapsed under the weight with a broken ankle. Until that day, I had assumed that "Pride goes before a fall" was just a trite expression.

Reflecting on that incident, I recognize several reasons why I fell, and I realize they are the same things that cause spiritual falls. Learn to recognize these stumbling blocks.

Stumbling Block 1: Pride

I didn't take the stairs or my load seriously enough, and I took myself much too seriously. When we're familiar with life's routine, we don't consider potential pitfalls. Pride convinces us that we are sufficient and independent. Proverbs 18:12 reminds us that "before his downfall a man's heart is proud, but humility comes before honor." That also goes for the female's heart that's obsessed with fashion! Clothing ourselves in humility protects us from falling, and a little humility is far less painful than a lot of humiliation.

Create an acronym with the word *pride* that describes your experience with this stumbling block.

P _____ R _____ I _____ D _____ E _____

Full of pride, I stumbled and fell. I learned to admit the cause, asked God to help me avoid it in the future, and was able to move forward with renewed confidence.

I'm reminded of two kings, David and Saul. Take time to read Saul's story in 1 Samuel 15, and then David's story in 2 Samuel 11. When you finish, complete the chart below.

	Evidence of pride in both stories	Results of their prideful actions
King Saul	_____	_____
King David	_____	_____

Both Saul and David had nasty falls, but it was their heart's response to their sin that determined whether they would get up. Unlike Saul, David's sin broke his heart. His prayer of repentance clearly reveals why he recovered from his fall.

"I know my transgressions, and my sin is always before me. Against you, you only, have I sinned and done what is evil in your sight, so that you are proved right when you speak and justified when you judge." **Psalm 51:3-4**

Read David's magnificent prayer of repentance in Psalm 51. What actions did David take after his fall (vv. 3-4)?

_____

David humbled himself and repented—he was a man after God's own heart (1 Sam. 13:14). If he felt it necessary to ask God to create in him a pure heart, how much more do we need to ask the same thing? We need cleansed hearts to choose the right path. Our feet will tread the paths our hearts pursue.

The bad news is: Sin can trip us up. The good news is: We can get up again, for "though a righteous man falls seven times, he rises again" (Prov. 24:16).

What would your life look like/be like if you were totally a woman after God's own heart? List at least 8 indicators.

1. _____   5. _____

2. _____   6. _____

3. _____   7. _____

4. _____   8. _____

How has pride interfered in these indicators of your spiritual journey?

_____

_____

What is God saying to you about the next steps you must take regarding these in your life?

_____

_____

We'll look at three more stumbling blocks tomorrow.

Day Four
More Stumbling Blocks, More Falls

Remember my prideful tumble down dormitory stairs? I identified four stumbling blocks from that experience; watching for these same stumbling blocks in my faith-walk has helped me strengthen my spiritual stride. We studied the first one in day 3—pride. The remaining three are the focus of today's study.

Stumbling Block 2: Priorities

I protected the wrong thing. My net worth was tied up in my clothes, but was it worth a broken ankle—especially since my treasure became a mangled mess at the bottom of the stairs? If my priority had been safety instead of vanity, the result of the fall would have been different, or perhaps I wouldn't have fallen at all.

"Be careful how you walk," the Apostle Paul warns us, "not as unwise men, but as wise" (Eph. 5:15, NASB). Check the spot that best represents your priorities:

●───●

Misplaced priorities   Right priorities
cause me to stumble.   direct my steps.

Offer a current example from your life to support your answer.

_____

How does Proverbs 3:5-6 help you with your life's priorities?

_____

We Christians often too glibly describe our priorities "God, family, church, work, and a little bit for me." This evening fill in the chart below referring only to today:

How I Spent My Time	How I Spent My Money
_____	_____
_____	_____
_____	_____
_____	_____

These represent your priorities! What insights can you gain about yourself, what you say is important to you, and what actually is important to you?

_____

_____

Stumbling Block 3: Preoccupation

In my rush to finish moving, I failed to practice disciplines that allow me to navigate safely—counting the stairs, holding the rails. Sometimes packed schedules and pressing demands set us up for a fall. Being busy, even with good things, can distract us from the best.

God commands us to " 'be still' " (Ps. 46:10) so we'll take time to know Him. When we do, the frenzied pace of life is less likely to lead to a fall. If we learn to schedule stillness into our lives, we'll find rest in the race as we count on Him, holding onto Him.

What were you focused on the last time you—

fought with someone close to you? _____

felt ineffective in your work? _____

resented another's success or high regard? _____

worried over time or money commitments? _____

In those situations, how often was your focus on seeking God's presence?

_____

Mark on the continuum how satisfied you are with your answer.

●———●

Dissatisfied   Satisfied   Very Satisfied

Stumbling Block 4: Pressure

I carried too much. I'd obviously forgotten how my blindness limits my ability to walk with an unusually heavy load. It's easier to keep our balance when we monitor the weight of our cargo.

We all need to measure how much we can carry in view of our life situations. Stress inevitably depletes us and leaves us vulnerable. Maintaining a sense of balance reduces our chance of falling and keeps our burdens light.

Read the Lord's invitation to you in Matthew 11:28-30. With your Bible open, pray these words to God, agreeing that you will come learn from Him and take His yoke.

Review days 3 and 4 by listing the four stumbling blocks you may encounter in your spiritual journey:

1. _____   3. _____

2. _____   4. _____

Learn to recognize and then avoid these stumbling blocks that will keep you from falling spiritually.

All the talk about running and races is exciting but exhausting. Managing routine tasks day in and day out tires most of us. The biblical exhortations we've studied seem to say, "Get in the race! Train! Strain to finish!" Goals that we often cannot approach, much less attain, can be daunting, even discouraging.

The disconnect between who we are and who we want to be is a prime stressor. The nagging discontent is built into our culture and rapidly changing times and undermines our confidence and competence. It often leaves us feeling guilty, second-rate, even like a failure. Such thoughts are debilitating to us physically, emotionally, mentally, spiritually, relationally—any way you might name.

FOR EXTRA CREDIT

The psalmist experienced similar mental defeats. Read the following verses in Psalms: 6:2-3; 31:7,9-12; 32:1-5; 38:3-10. How did he describe his thoughts and feelings about his life? I'll start you off with an example:

He is anguished; thinks his suffering will not end (6:3). _____

_____

How did he describe his physical response? I'll start you off again.

He is faint (6:2). _____

_____

Look back over the two lists. Circle the things you are thinking and feeling.

Thoughts are as powerful now as they were when King David penned his cries. It matters what we think, where our minds linger. No wonder the Apostle Paul insisted:

"Whatever is true, whatever is worthy of reverence and is honorable and seemly, whatever is just, whatever is pure, whatever is lovely and lovable, whatever is kind and winsome and gracious, if there is any virtue and excellence, if there is anything worthy of praise, think on and weigh and take account of these things [fix your minds on them]. Practice what you have learned ... and model your way of living on it, and the God of peace (of untroubled, undisturbed well-being) will be with you" (Phil. 4:8-9, AMP).

Offer a prayer to God, mentioning the things that are worthy of your thoughts.

Day Five
Where Are You Walking?

Granddaddy had several stout hunting dogs. On one visit, I tiptoed to the dog pen, opened the gate, and closed it quickly behind me. Were those dogs happy to see me! It was canine chaos! Those big hounds jumped on me, licked my face, and almost immediately knocked me flat on the ground. That's when I noticed a peculiar aroma.

"There is a way that seems right to a man but in the end it leads to death." **Proverbs 14:12**

Actually, it would have been hard not to notice, since I had fallen in it. The happy dogs were prancing all over me, and I was a smelly reminder that I had fallen in the wrong place.

We must wisely choose where we walk on our faith journey as well. Sometimes a path may appear harmless, but if you stumble, you might end up in quicksand.

A friend of mine used to enjoy Internet chat rooms. They seemed innocent enough—until she become emotionally involved with a fellow chatter and found herself sinking in the quicksand of adultery.

I'm not saying you should never chat on the Internet, but always be mindful of your weaknesses. A path that is harmless for one may be deadly for another. You can't become a chocoholic if you never taste chocolate, and it's impossible to get into credit card debt if you don't own those persuasive pieces of plastic.

What harmless things in your life take you where you do not want or need to go?

_____

The wisdom of Proverbs proclaims: "In the way of righteousness there is life; along that path is immortality" (Prov. 12:28). Here's what we learn along the way of righteousness:

1. Righteousness means we are declared right with God. All the demands of His holy law have been met. We have not met these demands; they have been met by Christ on our behalf. To walk in the way of righteousness means living life the way Jesus lived His.

Describe the life Jesus lived according to Romans 5:1-10 and Philippians 2:5-11.

_____

_____

2. God declares us guilt-free under the law because He accepts Christ's righteousness, His right standing with God, as the guarantee of our righteousness. This marvelous transaction is activated by one condition: our faith in Jesus Christ to make this so.

Read Romans 1:17; 3:25-26; 4:20,22; Galatians 2:16; and Philippians 3:8-11. Describe this faith which has made you righteous.

_____

_____

3. When we understand the love and forgiveness of God make us righteous, the natural consequence is to walk with gratitude and a deep desire to please and honor God. Our good choices don't bring us salvation, but they offer evidence of our salvation.

Read John 15:1-17; Romans 6:2-7,14; 7:6. Describe the life of one who is right with God.

_____

_____

Our righteousness is not dependent upon us. It's dependent on the One we're tied to: "We have this hope as an anchor for the soul, firm and secure" (Heb. 6:19).

Several years ago I found myself tied to a bungee cord and standing seven stories above common sense! When the platform attendant said, "Jump," I did! At first it was euphoric. I felt free, yet secure; weightless, yet strangely grounded. I actually liked it until the bungee stretched to its full extension and jerked me back to the inescapable reality that I was breaking the law of gravity and falling up!

Life is like bungee jumping. We fall down. We get up. The critical detail is: Where is the rope tied? I felt secure falling seven stories because I was tied to something immovable.

When Christ found us, we had already fallen, just as if we had jumped off a seven-story platform tied to nothing. We were doomed with no hope of recovery. Then His forgiveness acted like our bungee cord. He redeemed us and fastened us to Himself, wrapping us safely in the unbreakable cords of His great salvation.

Once we are fastened to Christ, our Heavenly Father lovingly guides us as we learn to walk with Him. Jude 24 assures us that He is a reliable companion, one we can hang on to as we travel life's journey: "To him who is able to keep you from falling and to present you before his glorious presence without fault and with great joy" (Jude 24).

In Jude 24, underline what God prevents, and circle how He presents us. What difference do these truths make in your life today?

My bungee jump wasn't the only time I've chosen to fall. It's difficult for sighted people to imagine what it is like to walk in the dark, to carry out daily routines, handle a career, or raise kids. I know, because I was once fully sighted. I understand both worlds.

Some days the weight of blindness falls heavily on me. Even simple things—wearing matching socks, reading the mail, clipping the baby's fingernails—feel like monumental challenges. Blindness feels stifling because it turns ordinary routines into extraordinary tasks and leaves me worn out. On those days my fatigue seems more powerful than my faith. Not even sheer grit is enough to propel me out of bed to face the day. So, guess what I do. Before I get up, I fall down ... in prayer. And you must, too.

Conclude this week's study in prayer. Kneel in God's presence. From this humble posture, thank Him for who He is and what He is doing in your life.

What is God saying to you about the sins and stumbling blocks in your spiritual path?

What is the significance of God's timing in revealing these truths to you?

What response will you make to God?

---

[1]John Piper, *A Hunger for God* (Wheaton, IL: Crossway Books, 1997), 14-15.

Listening Guide

1. Temptation has two things in common:

    • It's _____.

    • It's _____.

2. We must get rid of:

    • the _____

    • the _____ that so easily entangle us

3. Your falls on your faith journey can be prevented if you choose to _____ .

    • When you fall before Him in _____, you rise with

      the _____ of the Lord.

    • When you fall before Him in _____, you rise with _____.

    • When you fall before Him in _____, you rise with _____.

Remember God's Word

One cold January afternoon, our family had just returned to Springfield, Missouri, after a long, tiring drive. Before going home, we had to stop at the store, and as we pulled into the parking lot, it was all I could do to wait for the car to stop before I opened the door. The heat in our van had abandoned us about three hours from home and I was cold! As soon as Phil shut off the engine, I swung the door open and held on as it pulled me swiftly out of the van. By the time Phil and our oldest son, Clayton, had opened their doors, I was headed to the middle of the parking lot.

"Stop, Mom," Clayton yelled. "There's a car coming!" Phil ran over to me. "Why are you in such a hurry?" he asked.

Before I could answer, Clayton said, "Mom, you could have been hit by a car. That would've been awful!"

I was pleased with his concern and ashamed of my impetuousness. "You're right," I said. "That would have been awful."

"Yeah," Clayton continued. "Because if you died, Dad and I would never be able to find anything!"

Well, that was about the most accurate statement I'd ever heard!

My guys are fully sighted, but I'm still their eyes. They're constantly asking me, "Where's my …?" and "Have you seen my …?" Since they don't pay any attention to where they put things, it's easier for them to ask me than it is to search.

My world is pretty dark, so I must depend on my memory. If something is out of place, I can't access it, and it's as though it doesn't exist. I have to diligently maintain my closet, my pantry, and my refrigerator because I can't rely on others to find the chocolate chips when my hormones are screaming, "Feed me! Feed me!" And that's only the beginning. There are so many things I have to order and organize in my life—knowing that I can't always rely on someone being there to check if out for me visually. Do my socks match when I leave the house in the morning? They do if I've put them in the right place! I must rely completely on remembering where things are and maintaining good habits to keep them in the places I've memorized.

Relying on sight is OK … as long as we can see, but we all have times when life gets dark, times when we can't see. To shed light on our path, we have to know God's Word. Not just know where to find it, but know it! The psalmist put it this way: "I will delight in your principles and not forget your word" (Ps. 119:16, NLT).

Since I cannot rely on sight, I frequently listen to tapes. I treasure a recording of Corrie ten Boom speaking in a church. She shared with fellow believers that her family delighted in remembering God's Word during dark times—for them and for the world. When they were arrested (along with her cousin Peter) by Hitler's regime, they whispered to one another, "What do you have in your shoe, Corrie?" "What do you have in your shoe, Daddy?" "What do you have in your shoe, Betsy?"

What was in their shoes? Romans 8, 2 Corinthians 4, and Ephesians 1. They had torn pages from their Bibles and placed them in the soles of their shoes. Talk about standing on the promises! Even while confined to a concentration camp and enduring harsh conditions of hunger and abuse, they literally walked with the Word.[1]

None of us can be certain that we'll have access to a Bible just when we need it, and we can't rely solely on others, like our pastor or Bible-study teacher, to find the exact Scripture we need. If we don't discipline ourselves to memorize the truth, it won't be accessible when we reach for it. We must learn to remember the Scripture that will guide us when we can't see.

Memorizing the truth will allow the light of the World to illuminate even your darkest places with the radiance of His Word. If you remember God's Word, a good memory will see you through.

When we memorize God's Word, it becomes real to us—it becomes what we speak and what we stand on. It empowers us to do all things through Christ, regardless of circumstances. This week, I'm hoping to remind you of the vitality God's Word brings to your Christian journey and to inspire you to practice the discipline of Scripture memory.

"Fix these words of mine in your hearts and minds; tie them as symbols on your hands and bind them on your foreheads. Teach them to your children, talking about them when you sit at home and when you walk along the road, when you lie down and when you get up" (Deut. 11:18-19).

"Remember His wonders which He has done, His marvels, and the judgements uttered by His mouth" (Ps. 105:5, NASB).

"Just when I need You most, You hear me
Just when I least deserve, You rescue me
All of the times I've failed You
Just show Your promises to be true."[2]

Textbook Treasures

" 'The LORD your God is with you,
  he is mighty to save.
He will take great delight in you,
  he will quiet you with his love,
  he will rejoice over you with singing' "
(Zeph. 3:17).

"Love the LORD your God with all your heart
and with all your soul and with all your
strength. These commandments that I
give you today are to be upon your hearts.
Impress them on your children. Talk about
them when you sit at home and when you
walk along the road, when you lie down and
when you get up. Tie them as symbols on
your hands and bind them on your foreheads.
Write them on the doorframes of your houses
and on your gates" (Deut. 6:5-9).

"Great is the LORD and most worthy of praise;
  his greatness no one can fathom.
One generation will commend your work
  to another;
  they will tell of your mighty acts" (Ps. 145:3-7).

Prepare to enter the classroom:

This week, our study's focus is to remember. Glance now at the titles of the five days' study ... you'll feel encouraged from the outset about how powerfully your memory sustains and grows your faith.

This week, you begin practicing a prayer technique that helps you study, remember, meditate upon, and apply the truths of Scripture. Simply stated, this technique is to use the words of Scripture as your prayers. For example, after reading the first Textbook Treasure, your prayer might be: "Thank You, God, that You are always with me. I'm over-whelmed that You see and know everything about me, and Your response to all my failures and faith-lessness is delight, is quieting my noisy fears, is finding joy in me that You set to music! What an awesome God You are to me."

Practice this technique now so that your week's study begins with prayer. Read carefully all the verses in Textbook Treasures. Choose at least three meaningful verses or phrases to form a prayer to God. Consider writing your prayer to practice this technique.

Day One
Remember What Great Things the Lord Has Done

When I was a little girl, long before my eyes grew dim, I used to lie on the grass in my front yard and gaze at the sky. On those warm Florida afternoons, I stretched out under the oak tree and imagined amazing things in the clouds' shapes above me. I could see hammers and elves, trucks and teapots. Once I even saw Snow White and all seven dwarfs!

I still gaze heavenward into that vast blue canvas stretched out overhead, but now, even on the most brilliant days, all my eyes see is gray. Sometimes that makes me feel sad—until I remember the clouds. They still dance through my imagination to the music only my memory can play. Then I smile, for I have a treasure hidden in my memory that no eye disease can ever touch. I can stretch out in the front yard with my two sons and enjoy the pictures the clouds draw for them. Memory will sustain you even when sight won't serve you. That's why it's essential to remember what really matters.

> **Memory will sustain you even when sight won't serve you.**

The Bible says that when the children of Israel were in the wilderness, God "guided them with the cloud by day and with light from the fire all night" (Ps. 78:14).

What did the cloud represent in Exodus 24:15-17 and 33:7-11?

_____

Israel remembered the cloud that led them. They also surely remembered the difficulties of their wilderness journey. The desert was a place of longing and need, a place that required them to depend totally upon God.

Why did God allow His covenant people to wander in the desert for so long (Deut. 8:2)?

_____

What did Moses want the people to remember about God and His purposes in leading them through the wilderness?

_____

The Old Testament suggests that the harsh conditions of the wilderness revealed the true nature of the sojourners. They were grumblers and complainers in the immediate, daily presence of God! Their faith grew faint, and they often lost their perspective.

I believe God allows us to wander through deserts to test us. The wilderness shows who we are and whom we trust.

Remember a time when you felt as if you lived in a desert. What did God teach you there?

_____

When you think of your desert, remember the cloud that described God's presence. Throughout the Old Testament, the cloud is recalled so that Israel remembered the awesome God who led them and loved them. Remembering was a key discipline to strengthen Israel's faith. Remembering God's presence meant remembering God's activity.

" 'The LORD himself goes before you and will be with you; he will never leave you nor forsake you. Do not be afraid; do not be discouraged.' "

Deuteronomy 31:8

Match the references to the cloud in the left column with the appropriate description of God's activity from the list on the right.

___ 1. Exodus 14:19-20   a. Guiding Israel out of Egypt and through the wilderness

___ 2. Exodus 33:10   b. Signal to break up camp and move

___ 3. Exodus 40:36-37   c. A barrier between Israel and Egyptians

___ 4. Leviticus 16:2   d. Place of revelation; where God speaks

___ 5. Numbers 9:15-16   e. Way to summon the people to worship

___ 6. Nehemiah 9:12   f. God's presence over the mercy seat

___ 7. Psalm 99:7   g. Sustained, immediate, presence of God over the tabernacle

Circle phrases in the right column that describe what you seek from God's presence.

When the Israelites' wilderness journey ended, they still faced an uncertain future. Even though the cloud was no longer there to guide them, God was still there.

What does Deuteronomy 31:8 say about God's presence when life is uncertain or dark?

_____

Even when shadows darken our world, we'll see that God is with us if we look closely. His presence will always lead us to our promised land. So remember the great things the Lord has done and is doing. Then you'll never forget in the dark what you knew was true in the light. You'll be able to smile even when you see only gloom and shadows.

FOR EXTRA CREDIT:
Remember what matters from your week 1 study of faith.
1. What is faith?
2. What evidence of faith in your life have you seen since starting this study?
3. Jot down the most meaningful insight from week 1, either from the text or your study notes, and meditate on it again.
4. Record key scriptural phrases or verses to pray back to God.
5. Spend 10 minutes in prayer, using these scriptural truths. Remember the great things God has done for you.

(Answers to matching exercise: 1. C; 2. E; 3. B; 4. F; 5. G; 6. A; 7. D)

Day Two

Remember Your Light in the Darkness

For me, memory is more reliable than sight. One of the oddities of living with failing sight is that the changes are both sudden and subtle. Many times I've operated on the mistaken notion that I could see where I was going, only to realize—when I walked into a wall—that my sight had worsened. If I had made it a point to remember where the doorway was, I would have made it safely down the hall.

That's also true in a spiritual sense. Learning to trust God and walk by faith means learning to remember His Word. Knowing the Bible helps us to act on what we know is true rather than merely reacting to what we see.

None of us can be certain that we'll have access to a Bible just when we need it, and we can't rely solely on our pastor or Bible-study teacher to find the exact Scripture we need. If we don't discipline ourselves to memorize Scripture, it may not be accessible when we reach for it.

Suppose a job layoff, a car accident, or a serious illness were to shake your tranquil world. Life suddenly seems mercilessly dark. If you have memorized the truth that God will keep in perfect peace those whose minds are stayed on Him (Isa. 26:3), it can help you to react peacefully to these crises based on what you know to be true.

Does darkness threaten? Identify it and memorize what God says about your situation.

Aging   "Even to your old age and gray hairs I am he, I am he who will sustain you" (Isa. 46:4).

Grief   " 'Blessed are those who mourn, for they will be comforted' " (Matt. 5:4).

Fear   " 'Are not two sparrows sold for a penny? Yet not one of them will fall to the ground apart from the will of your Father. And even the very hairs of your head are all numbered. So don't be afraid; you are worth more than many sparrows' " (Matt. 10:29-31).

Guilt   "If anyone is in Christ, he is a new creation; the old has gone, the new has come!" (2 Cor. 5:17).

Loneliness   "God has said, 'Never will I leave you; never will I forsake you' " (Heb. 13:5).

Worry   "Cast all your anxiety on [God] because he cares for you" (1 Pet. 5:7).

Identify what threatens you in each of the three difficult situations you noted in week 1.

Situation 1:	❑ Aging	❑ Grief	❑ Fear	❑ Guilt	❑ Loneliness	❑ Worry
Situation 2:	❑ Aging	❑ Grief	❑ Fear	❑ Guilt	❑ Loneliness	❑ Worry
Situation 3:	❑ Aging	❑ Grief	❑ Fear	❑ Guilt	❑ Loneliness	❑ Worry

Use your Bible concordance or Internet search engine to learn what the Bible says about the word you've chosen for each situation. Record in your journal the scriptural references which relate most directly to your words.

Consider choosing one verse to memorize for each difficult situation.

Memorizing the truth will allow the Light of the world to illuminate even your darkest places with the radiance of His Word. If you remember what matters, a good memory will see you through.

Ask someone you know who practices memorizing Scripture the following questions:

1. How do you choose the verse you memorize?
2. What Bible translations do you memorize, and why?
3. Describe the practical steps that you take to remember Scripture.
4. What verse(s) are you currently memorizing?

Be prepared to share their answers in the group meeting.

FOR EXTRA CREDIT:
Remember what matters from your week 2 study of fears and faith.
1. What have you learned about the leader (Jesus Christ) you are following?
2. What evidence have you seen of your willingness to follow Jesus' leadership and model your life after His example since starting this study?
3. Jot down the most meaningful insight from week 2, either from the text or your study notes, and meditate on it again.
4. Record key scriptural phrases or verses to pray back to God.
5. Spend 10 minutes in prayer, using these scriptural truths. Remember the light God is shining into your difficulties and dark places through His Word.

Day Three
Remember Your Greatest Treasure

I'm sure you've asked yourself: How in the world does she put on makeup!? Someday in a power blackout, it might become important to you, too! So I'll reveal my secret. I do it through concentration and reinforcement.

My mother taught me the system years ago, and it involves counting. I know how many times to brush my blush brush against my blush palette (I dare you to read that out loud three times fast!), and exactly where and how many times to swish that brush along my cheekbone. The system works the same for all my cosmetics. It's very reliable as long as I concentrate and don't lose count. In fact, it's more reliable than looking in a mirror. With these habits, anyone can apply makeup during a full eclipse!

Here's the catch: My system is only reliable when I reinforce what I have memorized. If I didn't habitually practice what I've memorized, I'd soon forget. And the result wouldn't be pretty! The result of allowing God's truths to be forgotten due to mental laziness isn't pretty either.

> "I have hidden your word in my heart that I might not sin against you."
>
> **Psalm 119:11**

According to Psalm 119:11, what ugliness do we keep out of our lives through memorizing God's Word?

_____

The truths we find in God's Word are far more than precepts that help us not to sin; in and of themselves they are treasures worth preserving. Throughout Psalm 119, the writer uses phrases that say *I will remember,* and *I do not forget.* And guess what he's referring to? Yes, God's Word! He knew the value of remembering it.

Look at some of the things that are ours when we remember God's Word. Read the following verses, from Psalm 119, and fill in the blanks provided. God's Word ...

Verse 24 _____   Verse 98 _____   Verse 104 _____

Verse 28 _____   Verse 99 _____   Verse 156 _____

Verse 52 _____   Verse 103 _____   Verse 165 _____

See what a precious treasure you have in God's Word? Treat it like the treasure it is, and hide it in your heart. Make room for it on the tablet of your memory.

Many techniques can help us memorize Scripture. If you don't have one, here are some suggestions for developing the discipline of remembering your greatest treasure.[3]

1. Keep a record of verses to memorize. Use a notebook, computer data file, or index card box—anything to which you have easy access. Choose verses that speak to personal needs, that inspire devotion in your life, that give words to your prayers.

In this study, you've been encouraged to memorize a verse or passage each week. Anytime you participate in an organized Bible study, you have the opportunity to memorize Scriptures with common themes. What a wonderful way to learn the lessons of faith.

If you have not done so, go back to each week's Textbook Treasures. Choose a verse or passage to memorize. Start your memorization list, and make these five passages the first ones you enter. Continue this exercise with the following suggestions:

2. Find the verse you're memorizing in your Bible. Read it out loud, in its context of the passage or chapter. Underline it. Visualize it on the page. Rehearse its reference.

3. Write your memory verses on cards small enough to fit in your wallet (2x3 is a good size) or in the filing system you've selected. Include the Scripture's reference and the topic to which the Scripture relates as well.

4. Memorize! Look at the verse on your card; divide it into natural breaks. Learn the verse a phrase at a time, word for word. You might try recording the verse on tape, leaving blank tape after each verse so that you can repeat it out loud.

5. Set aside time to memorize and review verses you've memorized. Anytime a physical activity permits you to concentrate on a second task, memorize and review Scripture.

Choose now a set time each week for Scripture memory. Record your time here.

_____

Call your accountability partner. Explain what you've just done, and ask her to check on your progress for the next four weeks.

6. Review memorized verses regularly. This is key to Scripture memory. The following schedule will help you commit the Scriptures to long-term memory:

Once a day for six weeks,
Once a week for the next six weeks,
Once a month for life!

FOR EXTRA CREDIT:

Remember what matters from the week 3 study on choosing the right response.

1. Review your study notes about attitudes you need in order to receive difficult gifts. How do these lessons apply to your attitude about Scripture memory?
2. Since starting this study, what evidence have you seen of the discipline of rejoicing and gratitude?
3. Jot down the most meaningful insight from week 3, either from the text or your study notes, and meditate on it again.
4. Record key scriptural phrases or verses to pray back to God.
5. Spend 10 minutes in prayer, using these scriptural truths. Remember the joy God brings you and the gratitude He prompts in you through His Word.

Day Four
Reinforce Your Greatest Memory

Remember what you discovered yesterday, that God's Word is your greatest treasure. We prove how precious and valuable it is by how we act toward it. Memorizing Scripture is evidence of how much we treasure it. To maintain your wonderful memory work, you must frequently review what you've memorized, the focus of today's study.

A number of techniques can reinforce your Scripture memory. One way I keep my Scripture memory agile is to take cues from the clock. If I'm sitting down to hot tea and sugar cookies in the afternoon, I press my talking watch. If it says 3:23, I think of a verse with that address. Ah, Romans 3:23: "All have sinned and fall short of the glory of God." Or Colossians 3:23: "Whatever you do, work at it with all your heart, as working for the Lord, not for men." If I can't quote a verse with that time's address, I look it up in my Bible on tape and work on reciting it.

What time is it now? _____

What verse do you know, even partially, with this time's address? _____

How could this strategy for reinforcing Scripture memory work for you?

_____

Our family also uses Scripture cards at the dinner table. We read one each night and take turns reciting it.

We can memorize anything if we concentrate on it and reinforce it. Then it becomes near to us, and we act on what we have memorized. " 'The word is very near you, in your mouth and in your heart, that you may do it' " (Deut. 30:14, NKJV). If I can do it with cosmetics, you can do it with God's Word!

Recall an incident when you read or heard a Scripture verse and realized how much you needed it on a difficult day prior to that.

_____

_____

Circle on a scale of 1-10, with 1=no hope and 10=completely hope-filled, how hopeful you are that the words of Deuteronomy 30:14 can be true for you.

1   2   3   4   5   6   7   8   9   10

> "I can do all things through Christ who strengthens me."
>
> **Philippians 4:13, NKJV**

The Rothschild family has one more secret for reinforcing Scripture memory. It's our family's personal, two-number code, and it contains all we need to have a power-packed day. The two numbers are 4 and 13. When Clayton and Connor leave for school in the morning, I'll call out, "4-13." When I'm feeling overwhelmed, Clayton will respectfully say, "4-13 it, Mom." When Phil has a major project due at work, I'll remind him, "4-13, honey." When Connor has a toddler meltdown in the candy aisle at the grocery store, I … pay $4.13 to the cashier to get him quiet! Just kidding on that one!

You may have already guessed that 4-13 stands for the well-known verse in Philippians, "I can do all things through Christ who strengthens me" (NKJV). For us, that verse is an awesome reminder that the power and presence of Christ in our lives means nothing is too big, too hard, too puzzling, or too overwhelming to warrant an "I can't" attitude.

Often, parents choose a life verse for children when they are born—a verse that expresses hopes and prayers for their children's lives and their faith.

Do you have a life verse, something as powerful for you as Philippians 4:13 is for the Rothschild family? If not, spend a few minutes reviewing this workbook or noting verses you've highlighted in your Bible. Choose a life verse for this time in your life and put into practice the six steps for memorizing Scripture we learned in day 3.

Never forget that the important things sealed in your memory are never lost. So spend time memorizing what matters and maintaining what you've memorized. When it's dark and you can't see, God will become your vision if His truths are hidden in your heart.

Most of all, remember where we started our remembering—with the Lord and His great activity in the world and in our lives. He never forgets you. You are always on His mind and in His thoughts. He remembers what matters—you!

So by day or by night, make Him your best thought, and make sure you remember to thank Him for His Word and His goodness to you. "Remember His wonders which He has done, His marvels and the judgments uttered by His mouth" (Ps. 105:5, NASB).

FOR EXTRA CREDIT:
Review the verses you've worked to memorize during the five weeks of this study. If you haven't been memorizing, then read over, review, and meditate on the verses you chose yesterday to start your Scripture memory file.

Use the words and phrases of these Scriptures to pray back to God, thanking Him that His Word is alive. Even better, thank Him that He is the living Word.

Day Five
Remember the God Who Delights in You

My friend Joni's daughter came home from school after a long day of testing. Hannah was a first-grader, and this was her first experience with standardized tests.

"Well, Hannah," Joni asked, "how did the tests go?"

Hannah's response was tentative. "Fine," she said. "Except that … well … Mom, I think I got an F in sex." Hannah added that the teacher came by and marked an F under her name next to the word *sex*.

"Honey," Joni said. "The F stands for female—not fail! They wanted to know whether you're a girl or a boy. You're a girl, so your sex is female."

Hannah heaved a sigh of relief, and they both began to laugh.

What a perfect illustration of what it's like to be human! We do what is required of us, giving it our best shot. Asked how we're doing, most of us cautiously respond, "Fine … I think I'm doing fine." Then … wham! A big F—failure! Even small failures knock the wind out of our self-esteem, making us feel silly or stupid. Regardless of the size of the mistake, laughter, our good humor, the delight we have in life—these are wise, healthy responses. Archbishop Edward McCarthy once said that the ability to laugh at ourselves is a sign of maturity in our faith. Why is it, then, that it's so hard to laugh at ourselves? A couple of reasons: (1) we tend to take ourselves too seriously, and (2) we tend to give more weight to others' opinions of us than to God's opinion of us. That's why we've looked at the importance of memorizing and meditating on God's Word this week. When we remember His truth, it guides us. When we know His opinion of us from His Word, it matures and frees us from taking ourselves too seriously.

Think of a recent example when—

you took yourself too seriously: _____

you were too focused on others' opinions of you: _____

In those experiences, did you feel humbled or humiliated? Explain your answer.

_____

_____

Do you feel like hiding when these things happen? I know I do. But I recall the psalmist's words: "You are my hiding place; you will protect me from trouble and surround me with songs of deliverance" (Ps. 32:7). So go ahead and hide—in God! When we are hidden in Him, we experience great benefit.

According to the following verses, who are you in God, or what do you have in Him?

Acts 17:28 _____

1 Corinthians 1:5_____

2 Corinthians 5:21_____

Ephesians 2:21-22 _____

Ephesians 3:12 _____

Choose one of these "in Him" truths that you need today. Write it on a note card and tape it to your bathroom mirror. Each time you see your reflection this week, read your verse and ask God to allow that truth to be reflected in you.

Realize that your sense of self is derived from God's opinion of you, and that delivers you from fear of others' opinions of you. No matter how many embarrassing mistakes we make, God's opinion of us never changes. God doesn't want our self-worth to be based on how others perceive us or on what we see in the mirror. Instead, God's design is that our self-esteem rest securely on how He perceives us and on what we see in the mirror of His Word. Healthy self-esteem comes from God's esteem of us.

Reread the preceding paragraph. What amazing truths! How would you paraphrase this paragraph so that your closest friend would grasp its meaning? Write your thoughts here.

_____

_____

Regardless of what others say about you and what you think about yourself, remember what God says about you.

Find the references below; then fill in the blanks. As you fill in each one, pause and say out loud, "Thank You, God!" or offer your own cry of gratitude.

Remember what God says about you.

1 Samuel 12:22: You will never _____.

Isaiah 43:1: You are His _____.

Isaiah 43:4: You are _____.

Jeremiah 31:3: You are loved _____.

Romans 15:7: You are _____ by the Beloved.

1 Corinthians 6:20: You were _____ at great price.

2 Corinthians 5:17: You are a _____.

Ephesians 1:4: You were _____ to be _____.

Ephesians 2:10: You are His _____ created for a great purpose.

Philippians 3:9: You are defined by _____.

1 Peter 2:9: You are _____.

Do you see how serious God is about you? David was astounded by that realization. Read Psalm 8:3-5 and paraphrase it to express your wonder, too.

_____

_____

Can you even fathom the truth that the God of the universe clothed Himself in human flesh to come find you because He loved you and knew you were lost?

Many thoughts can dictate your perceptions and opinions. The opinions of others will shackle you. The chains of pride prohibit true liberty. But truth of what God says about you is worth remembering. The greatest truth of the ages is that God Himself stooped and came to us so that we would know the truth and the truth would set us free.

FOR EXTRA CREDIT:
Remember what matters from your week 4 study on running with endurance.
1. Review your study notes about confessing sin. How do these lessons apply to your study today about delighting in your life because God delights in you?
2. What evidence have you seen of overcoming the stumbling blocks mentioned in week 4, days 3 and 4 since starting this study?
3. Jot down the most meaningful insight from week 4, either from the text or your study notes, and meditate on it again.
4. Record key scriptural phrases or verses to pray back to God.
5. Spend 10 minutes in prayer, using these scriptural truths. Remember God's delight in you (Zeph. 3:17) and His wonderful promise that your name is recorded in His book of life (Luke 10:20).

[1] As recorded on "The Hiding Place" (Santa Ana: Vision House Publishers, 1974).
[2] Words and Music by Jennifer Rothschild © 1990 Rothschild Music (ASCAP)
[3] Adapted from "Guide to Memorizing Scripture" in _Disciple's Study Bible_ (Nashville: Holman Bible Publishers, 1988), 1780.

Listening Guide

1. When _____ will not serve you, _____ will sustain you.

2. God's mirror—His Word—is a flawless _____ of _____.

3. God's Word is the only _____ that is reliable to _____

   against the lies of the enemy.

4. The very Son of God fought with the weapon of the Word. In Matthew 4 Jesus'

   response to Satan three times used the three words, _____.

5. Regardless of how dark it may be, God's Word will _____ your vision.

Wait on God

A prison chaplain asked me to come to her Bible study one Saturday afternoon to provide music for the inmates who attended. I was uncomfortable from the start; but after I was thoroughly frisked and my keyboard was almost disassembled, I was really nervous! I had no idea what to expect.

I set up my keyboard, and the guard ushered in about 20 quiet women. No introductions were offered. The chaplain told me, "Go ahead and start." I began just as I would have in a church setting where everyone was eagerly responsive. Well, that went over about as well as an opera singer at a hoedown! I quickly sensed that I needed another approach. So I took a giant leap of faith and blurted out, "What would you like to sing?"

Silence. Then a gruff voice called out, "Just As I Am!"

"You mean the old hymn?" I asked. I was a little surprised; in my experience, this wasn't a song even church women enjoyed but rather endured at the service's end while they gathered their Bibles and purses and made covert plans for lunch.

The chaplain jumped in. "Jennifer, this is Sandy. She's been here for several years ..."

"For manslaughter," Sandy added, finishing the sentence.

"Yes," the chaplain continued, "and since she came to Christ, 'Just As I Am' has been her favorite song."

Very moved, I played the introduction, and as we began to sing, the weeping also began. Sandy was so overcome with emotion that she couldn't voice the words, and the chaplain pulled out a tissue and began to wipe away her own tears.

I've never heard "Just As I Am" sung more sweetly. I've never felt the words, "Just as I am, without one plea" more deeply. These women knew what it meant to plead before judge and jury. They understood what it meant to be declared guilty.

I realized how little I knew and understood about my own guilt and pardon. I also had trouble singing the words that day because I, too, wept. Just like Sandy, I was guilty "without one plea, But that Thy blood was shed for me."[1]

Knowing how much we are forgiven and embracing how much we are loved brings tears of gratitude from our hearts to our eyes. On the day we are released from our earthly shackles and stand before our Lord, He will lovingly cup each of our faces in His gentle hands and wipe every tear from every face once and for all. Until that day, our tears allow us to feel His touch every time we cry out to Him.

Textbook Treasures:
"The righteous cry and the LORD hears,
 And delivers them out of all their troubles.
 The LORD is near to the brokenhearted,
 And saves those who are crushed in spirit"
 (Ps. 34:17-18, NASB).

"As for me, I watch in hope for the LORD,
 I wait for God my Savior;
 my God will hear me" (Mic. 7:7).

Prepare to Enter the Classroom:
Pray phrases from Textbook Treasures to God. We all wait for our faith to become sight. Let's choose to live a life that's meaningful in the meantime. Successful waiting depends on knowing the God to whom you cry out, experiencing His responses to your cries, and understanding what is really worth waiting for.

Skim this book; record in your journal what you've learned about God, faith, and yourself. Share these truths with your accountability partner.

Day One
The Wisdom to Wait

The way I see it, there are three kinds of waiters—and I don't mean those serving at a banquet! Perhaps you'll recognize yourself in one of them.

First, the worried waiter wrings her hands and paces the floor. She calls her friends to bemoan her circumstances but forgets to take them to God in prayer.

Then the wishful waiter never lives in the present because her energy is tied to "what if" and not to "what is." She spends most of her time speculating on what it will be like when the wait is over, and until then she aimlessly gets through each day.

Finally, the wise waiters focuses on God's face, not on His hand—not on what He will do for her, how He will take care of her situation, or when He will end her wait. She is waiting only on God, and she is present, peaceful, and productive.

What kind of waiter are you?
❏ I'm present where I am.
❏ I'm wringing my hands.
❏ I'm waiting on God alone.
❏ I pine away over things that are not.
❏ I'm bending my knees.
❏ I'm waiting for the wait to end.

Many of us live in the meantime, waiting for something we want or need: a better job, less stress, a newer car. We endure the wait, and then the prize is awarded—only to find a new need, a new wait, and a new prize pop up in its place.

The prize is often what keeps us faithful while we wait, but consider that our joy isn't reserved for the awards ceremony, that there is something deeply joyful in the in-between time. If we focus on the prize alone, we'll see the waiting as a trial, missing the joy of the journey and overlooking the treasures along the way. Learning to wait teaches us that our joy doesn't depend on whether we get those things for which we've waited. It teaches us to experience the strengthening effect of *in-all joy*, not just *end-all joy*.

"Delight yourself in the LORD and he will give you the desires of your heart."

Psalm 37:4

So what do we do to make the meantime meaningful? (Psalm 37:4 is a wonderful answer.)

_____

When I delight in my husband, I am mindful of and interested in his desires. In fact, they become my desires. Without delighting in him, I would never spend three long hours sipping coffee at his favorite bookstore, surrounded by books I can't read and coffee I don't drink! But I do delight in him, so I want to be there and sip right along with him.

Consider the following synonyms for _delight_. Write beside each one the people, places, things, and delights in your life that come immediately to mind.

Gratified with _____   Enchanted by _____

Pleased when _____   Happy because_____

Satisfied with _____   Enraptured with_____

We mistakenly conclude that if we delight in God, He will give us what we want. But the emphasis should be on our delighting, not His giving. When we delight in God, He places in us the desires He wants us to have. "It is God who works in you," Paul reminds us, "to will and to act according to his good purpose" (Phil. 2:13). When our delight is in God, our desires will be what He wants for us instead of what we want for ourselves.

What you desire reflects where you delight. List your heart's desires honestly.

_____

_____

If you are delighting in God, your heart's desires reflect His heart's desire. Does your list reflect God's heart—or your own?   ❑ God's heart   ❑ My heart

God desires peace and contentment for all of His children. The more I delight in Him, the more that becomes my heart's desire. Yes, healing my eyes would be an extraordinary prize, but I would ultimately lose if I were physically whole but spiritually incomplete. Without peace and contentment, the joy of healing would be fleeting and shallow, but resting contentedly in Him provides a depth of grace which I will enjoy in His eternal presence.

Estimate on the scale below how closely your heart's desires align with the desire of God's heart.

●——●

Not on the same scale   Growing closer   Almost aligned   Perfectly aligned

What does Psalm 62:5-6 say you receive from God while you wait?

_____

My deep desire for peace and contentment comes from the heart of the God in whom I delight—a treasure He gives me while I wait in all of life's meantimes. Align your heart with God's, and your desires will reflect His—a delightful task to last a lifetime.

Read Philippians 2:3-8. What is the key to delighting in the things in which God delights?

_____

Use Philippians 2:3-8 to express to God what robs you of peace and contentment. Ask Him to illuminate the mind of Christ in you so you will desire His good purposes.

Day Two
Waiting and Hoping

One night, my friend Lori and I were returning home from a prayer conference. Usually I face my blindness with resolve, but this night was different. Still moved by what transpired at the conference, we began to discuss why God had not healed me. Was that His will? Was my sin or lack of faith holding back His healing? Didn't it reflect poorly on God that I was not healed?

Feelings like these aren't easily expressed, much less resolved; we finally agreed to explore them further when our bodies and spirits weren't so weary. I asked Lori to read Psalm 63 before she walked me in. By the dim light she read: " 'My soul waits in silence for God only' ... Oh!" she said, "that's Psalm 62, not 63!"

"Read it again," I said, "that's the best mistake you ever made." "My soul, wait in silence for God only, For my hope is from Him. He only is my rock and my salvation, My stronghold; I shall not be shaken" (Ps. 62:5-6, NASB).

In my painful questioning, those words drew me closer to God. He told me that my hope for healing is in Him alone. Therefore, my soul can wait as long as it takes, even through all my life on earth. He alone—not my healing—is my rock and my refuge. My deliverance from blindness is not my source of hope ... He is!

Life is full of hard questions. Find a word or phrase in Psalm 62–63 that applies to your difficult life questions—

about your daily work: _____   about your family: _____

about your finances: _____   about your future: _____

When we pin our hopes on the fulfillment of *our* desires, we fall into the trap of wishful waiting. We can't know whether our desires will be fulfilled. Even if we could, we set ourselves up for disappointment when our focus is on our desires instead of on God.

What was James' advice for wishful waiters (Jas. 4:14-15)?

_____

What does the psalmist desire for those who seek God (Ps. 40:16)?

_____

Describe when you most recently sought God in an attitude of joy and gladness.

_____

What do those seeking God and praising God love (Ps. 40:16)?

_____

When our hope is in God alone, He is our prize. That's what Paul meant when he wrote, "I press on toward the goal to win the prize for which God has called me heavenward in Christ Jesus" (Phil. 3:14). Paul's desire was God's desire, his prize was Christ's will for him, and his hope was in God. Trust produces hope in difficult times (see Ps. 22:4-5). If you're a wishful waiter, learn to trust the One who leads you through long waits, just as He led His rebellious people on their way to the promised land. Don't daydream about the milk and honey, just enjoy His manna. Place your hope in God; delight in Him, and you will never be disappointed.

God urges those who are wishful or worried to "call upon Me in the day of trouble; I shall rescue you, and you will honor Me" (Ps. 50:15, NASB). His prescription for the worried waiters is: "Do not be anxious about anything, but in everything, by prayer and petition, with thanksgiving, present your requests to God" (Phil. 4:6). If you do, "the peace of God, which transcends all understanding, will guard your hearts and your minds in Christ Jesus" (v. 7).

Day Three
Waiting When Your Soul Cries

Tears are the outward manifestation of inward emotions such as sorrow, pain, anger, or even joy. These emotions often fill our times of waiting, our despairing questions of "Why?" "How long?" and "For what purpose?" In waiting times, tears often flow.

Tears promote the health of the human eye. In the same way, soul-tears—crying out to God—contribute to the health of our souls. Realize that God has spiritual as well as physical purposes for your cries. Not one tear is physically shed or spiritually cried in vain.

Sometimes life hurts! When it does, we must admit our pain. We must learn to cry, not only in the physical act of shedding tears but also in allowing ourselves honest, heartfelt responses of sorrow or grief when those are warranted.

Crying is as individual as each personality. Some cry over coffee commercials, others don't cry at funerals. To experience the life of faith, we must abandon our pride and humbly admit our sorrow, pain, and needs. To be tenderly accepting of our own humanity allows us to cry out; when we do, we feel the strengthening hand of our Mighty God.

1. Tears cleanse

Tears wash debris off the surface of the eye. One tiny grain of sand causes tears to gush. God has created a wonderful process to cleanse your eyes—your tears.

He has also created an amazing process to cleanse your soul. I call it shedding soul-tears—allowing yourself to cry out to God in prayer from the bottom of your heart. Throughout the Psalms, we hear the sound of David's soul-tears as he cries out to God.

Note a situation in which David's soul-tears to God convey yours as well.

Psalm 5:1-2: _____

Psalm 109:2-4: _____

Psalm 145:18-19: _____

Sometimes life's winds blow hard. Harsh words, rejection, and cruelty allow debris to lodge in our hearts. We need to cry—to allow soul-tears to cry out from our heart to God's. He may not remove the difficulty, but crying out to Him invites Him to wash away devastating debris that could obstruct our view of Him as we wait to see His way.

Take time to meditate, rest, and listen to God. What debris is He washing from your life?

_____

2. Tears protect

One year, Connor and I displayed our patriotism by planting small flags in the front yard. We had no sooner finished planting the first pole than he quickly jerked it out of the ground. I was bent over him, so the jagged end of the flagpole jammed into my open eye.

Wham! It was definitely a patriotic moment—I saw stars and stripes forever! I had a scratched cornea, and for several days my eye produced enough tears to dehydrate my whole body. But the doctor said this was the best thing for my injury, because physical tears have an antibacterial effect on the eye that protects it from infection.

When our soul cries to God, we receive the same kind of protection, for we invite the Great Physician to protect us from spiritual infection. Let's look at two: bitterness and guilt.

What does Hebrews 12:14-15 caution us not to let grow?
❑ Weeds   ❑ Bitter root   ❑ Infection

What will you change based on the convicting words of Ephesians 4:30-32?

_____

If we cry out to God over a broken heart or hurtful quarrel, bitterness cannot become deeply rooted in us or spread beyond us.

Examine your heart. Has bitterness taken root there?   ❑ Yes   ❑ No
Are you willing to ask God to pull it out by the roots?   ❑ Yes   ❑ No

If He did, what might you expect? Meditate on Psalm 73:21-28 as you answer.

_____

David's soul cried out because of guilt. What were the results of his guilt (Ps. 38:4-8)?

_____

"I wait for you, O LORD;

you will answer, O Lord

my God."

Psalm 38:15

Notice the psalmist describes his guilt like lost health! David's cries emanated from his sin, not his circumstances. The painful physical symptoms he suffered convince me of this: sin intensifies the pain in our circumstances to the point that it feels unbearable.

What was the psalmist's positive choice in Psalm 38:15?

_____

Here's that word again—waiting! While you wait, cry tears of guilt to God over regrettable choices—sin—so that guilt cannot grow into depression, anxiety, or shame. Cry to God the tears only your soul can produce; it will bring healing as you release everything to Him.

Your difficult emotions put your spiritual health at risk. According to David's address to a large crowd in Psalm 32:1-7, what are the effects of sin and forgiveness?

Effects of sin   Effects of forgiveness

_____   _____

_____   _____

_____   _____

Are you astounded, as I am, by the strong links between physical and spiritual health? The medical community has discovered this truth and is paying attention to patients' needs for forgiving and being forgiven in order to maintain and improve health—truths that David experienced and described thousands of years ago!

How long has it been since your journey of faith took you down the Roman Road? This path not only leads to salvation but also to repentance, confession, and restoration of health for Christians. Summarize the truth in each of the following Scriptures.

Romans 3:23:_____   Offer God your

Romans 6:23:_____   repentance,

Romans 5:6-11:_____   and seek His

Romans 10:9-10:_____   healing of

Romans 8:31-39:_____   your soul.

I've struggled to handle all the emotions that accompany blindness—frustration, anger, loss, and sadness. God has tenderly taught me to cry to Him, to release my sorrow, and to be strengthened by those tears and cries.

Because I had misunderstood the purpose of tears, this lesson was vital. I mistakenly assumed that tears undermined my strength. The phrase *reduced to tears* makes crying

God longs for us to roll the burden of our emotions onto Him.

sound as if it weakens us and makes us smaller, but that's not true. Releasing sorrow to God doesn't lead to weakness; it generates supernatural strength. Crying never washes away our hope; it helps cleanse the eyes of our souls so we can clearly see the source of our hope.

I'm learning that allowing myself to feel the weight of painful emotions—allowing myself to cry out to God—enables me to roll the burden of those emotions onto Him. Believe that He longs to do the same for you.

Day Four

Waiting with Jesus

I take great solace in the shortest verse in the Bible, "Jesus wept" (John 11:35). His tears appear in the context of a powerful story about Jesus' beloved friend, Lazarus of Bethany, and his sisters, Mary and Martha.

Read the full story in John 11:1-44 and list every instance of waiting.

_____

_____

Which word best describes how Mary and Martha perceived the timing of Jesus' arrival in Bethany?

❑ Haphazard   ❑ Hurried   ❑ Timely   ❑ Too late
❑ Inconsiderate   ❑ Comforting   ❑ Discomforting

What purpose was served by the sickness and death of Lazarus (vv. 4,40)?

_____

What would Jews of Bethany have been taught about seeing the glory of God (Ex. 33:17-23)?

_____

One commentator said that the glory of God is the weight or importance of God, the light in which God confronts us as humans to make visible the invisible God.

To behold the glory of God meant certain death, but with the coming of Christ, the weight, the importance, the overwhelming nature of God Himself became visible to us—

and brought life! God's people had waited thousands of years. Nothing was more magnificent than the visibility of the invisible God.

What was Martha's greeting to Jesus in John 11:21?

_____

And what was Mary's echoing assumption in verse 32?

_____

John tells us what happened next: "When Jesus saw her weeping, and the Jews who had come along with her also weeping, he was deeply moved in spirit and troubled. 'Where have you laid him?' he asked. 'Come and see, Lord,' they replied" (vv. 33-34). And the startling, comforting two-word verse follows: "Jesus wept" (v. 35).

Two of Jesus' closest friends and faithful followers had missed the greatest teaching He could bring to them. Rather than rebuking their misunderstanding, Jesus closely attended their sorrow and outwardly expressed His own loss and grief. What an amazing God!

You and I are no different than Mary and Martha. We all grieve. We miss the glory of God when we walk by sight and seem to only see bitterness or difficulty. Jesus understands our sorrow. Beyond that, He is moved by our sadness and grief, so trust Him with your tears. They are precious to God.

How does Psalm 56:8 confirm that our tears are precious to God?

_____

> "You keep track of all my sorrows. You have collected all my tears in your bottle. You have recorded each one in your book."
>
> **Psalm 56:8, NLT**

Luke tells us Jesus also wept coming down from the Mount of Olives, approaching Jerusalem. "As he approached Jerusalem and saw the city, He wept over it" (Luke 19:41). Jesus' gaze extended beyond Jerusalem's beauty and into the future. He knew that within decades Jerusalem would lie in ruins—its beloved temple demolished, its commerce destroyed, its citizens dead or dispersed. He saw the needless, self-inflicted suffering of those who rebel against God's will—and He wept.

I think the same is true today. God looks into our hearts, sees the pain we have inflicted on ourselves by resisting Him and His gracious will—and He weeps.

Which of the actions listed below do you most need from God today?

❏ Comfort for your wounded soul ❏ Healing for your broken heart

❏ His loving guidance ❏ Assurance of His presence

It would be difficult to trust our tears to One who never cried. But "we do not have a high priest who is unable to sympathize with our weaknesses" (Heb. 4:15). Knowing that Jesus wept ministers to our soul's deepest needs.

There's another side to that coin, however. Have you ever thought that our tears can also minister to Jesus? Come see ... at a dinner in the courtyard of a rich Pharisee named Simon. Such homes of wealthy folks were often built around a square courtyard, and when a rabbi came to dine, many people would come to learn from him. That explains why a certain woman was at Simon's house that day. Luke calls her an "immoral woman" (7:37, NLT); most likely, she was a prostitute.

Jesus was reclining at the table. The woman approached Him with a precious alabaster container. She wanted to honor Jesus by anointing Him with the perfume in it; overcome, she began to weep. Her tears fell upon His feet, and she lovingly began to kiss them, pour the perfume on them, and wipe them with her hair.

What a beautiful picture of abandoned love! For a Jewish woman to loose her hair in public was very immodest. Even a prostitute would feel so, for she was in a religious man's home and in the presence of Jesus. She seems to have forgotten about everything but Jesus.

Read Jesus' words in Luke 7:44-48. Describe what the woman's tears meant to Jesus.

_____

What makes this scene so striking is the contrast between Simon and the woman. Although it was customary for the host to wash the feet of a guest, to give him the kiss of peace, and to anoint his head with a drop of attar of roses, Simon had done none of those things. When Jesus reminded him by saying, " 'Do you see this woman?' " (v. 44). He was saying, *Do you see this woman in contrast to you?*

The parable Jesus tells in verses 40-43 makes the contrast plain. Read this parable and restate its meaning as if Jesus had spoken directly to you.

_____

Each of us probably looks a lot like either Simon or the woman. Some of us, like Simon, are religious, good, and moral. We invite Jesus in and are enlightened by His teachings, but we remain unmoved by His presence. We spread before Him all our achievements and wealth, much like Simon spread the meal before Jesus. Simon seemed to be pretty impressed with himself. He thought he looked good in the eyes of man and God. Since he was obviously oblivious to spiritual needs in his life, he felt little love for Jesus.

Simon's self-sufficiency kept him from really knowing the One with whom he dined, but the woman was overwhelmed with her needs. This opened the door to the forgiveness and love of God. Surely that's why she cried tears of gratitude. They were the outward sign that she had totally abandoned herself to Him inwardly. The woman left Simon's house intimately connected to Jesus.

> We need the presence of God more than God needs our efforts to be good.

Do you allow religion to be a shallow substitute for experiencing the presence of Jesus? ❑ Yes ❑ No   Why or why not?

_____

God is moved by your tears of repentance, gratitude, and love. He is pleased and honored when you abandon yourself to Him because you trust Him, so cry out to Him.

Review these precious truths:
1. Our spiritual tears cleanse and protect our souls.
2. Jesus grieved with Mary and Martha when Lazarus died.
3. Jesus wept over Jerusalem because He saw its citizens' self-inflicted suffering leading to the destruction of their land.
4. We can trust our tears to Jesus who is able to sympathize with our weaknesses.
5. It is possible to be good, religious, and moral and still remain unmoved by the presence of Jesus.

Review the verses from weeks 1-5 that you memorized. Identify a verse from this week's study to commit to memory. Accountability partners can help us with our commitments. Call your partner and pray for one another.

Day Five
Worth the Wait: When Faith Becomes Sight

Moses is highlighted in the hall of faith (Hebrews 11) among other faith heroes. Each is mentioned for different reasons, but they share in common that they "were all commended for their faith, yet none of them received what had been promised" (v. 39).

We see the conclusion to Moses' journey of faith to the promised land on Mount Nebo.

Read about Moses' final moments in Deuteronomy 34:1-6. What did Moses see from the mountaintop?

Moses didn't get to see the walls of Jericho fall, ushering the Israelites into the long-awaited promised land. He never entered the land of milk and honey. God gave Moses only a glimpse of the land toward which he had journeyed for 40 years. But that wasn't the final mountain upon which Moses stood.

Mark 9:2-4 shows us Moses at the top of another mountain. What did Moses see there?

Moses missed out on the promised land from Mount Nebo, but guess where Moses was standing at the very moment when Christ was glorified before his eyes. Moses finally set foot onto the very plot of land he had been promised so many years before. Don't miss the amazing significance of this moment of glory. The mount of transfiguration was located among the dusty hills of Canaan, the land of promise. Moses had hoped for this land and now, at last, there he stood, face-to-face with the promised One in the promised land. Who could be satisfied with mere milk and honey when the sweetness of God stands before you?

> "Let us hold unswervingly to the hope we profess, for he who promised is faithful."
>
> **Hebrews 10:23**

Circle in the margin the word in Hebrews 10:23 that refers to the way we should hold onto our hope. Then underline the word that describes God's trustworthiness.

Just like Moses, our faith will become sight, and we too will see Him face-to-face. I don't know what it's like any more to look into people's faces. It's been many years since I saw a face clearly. As a child I looked into my mother's face, with its olive skin, and I looked into the sweetness of my dad's dancing blue eyes and watched his forehead wrinkle when he was in thought. I looked into the freckled faces of my sometimes annoying, but always adorable, brothers, and I looked into the wise eyes of my beloved grandparents. What fascinates me is that even though I know I saw all those precious faces, in my memory they are now draped in shadows, blurred and indistinguishable. It's a strange phenomenon. Even so, it excites me—because unless God chooses to heal me here on earth, the very first face I'll see with clarity will be the face of Jesus. That will be my ultimate reward. However, there are rewards we can enjoy now while we are still walking by faith, believing what we can't see.

Read John 20:24-29. What was Thomas' response in verse 25 when the other disciples told him they had seen Jesus?

_____

You don't have to see it to believe. In fact, there is great reward for those who choose to believe without seeing.

Listed below are some rewards offered as we walk by faith. Match the corresponding Scripture reference with its promised reward.

1. I have inexpressible and glorious joy.	John 20:29
2. God is not ashamed of me; He prepares a city for me	1 Corinthians 13:12
3. I am blessed because I believe.	Hebrews 11:13-16
4. I will see face-to-face and know as I am known.	1 Peter 1:8

Based on these verses, write in your journal a thankful prayer to our faithful God.

I'll always remember how Mike, my mobility instructor, wrapped up my first lesson of learning to walk in the dark. After he had walked me around my neighborhood, he pointed out some blooming hibiscus on the corner near my home. "When you smell the flowers," he said, "you know you're almost home."

Each of us will someday smell the flowers and know we're almost home. You see, our faith really will become sight. Right now, we believe what we cannot see, but a time will come when we will see what we have believed just like Moses did.

According to Deuteronomy 34:10, how did the Lord know Moses?
❑ Through a glass darkly   ❑ Face-to-face   ❑ From a distance

God had known Moses face-to-face all his life. But when Moses' faith became sight, Moses then knew God face-to-face. My dear friend, that's why we walk by faith, "the surpassing greatness of knowing Christ Jesus my Lord, for whose sake I have lost all things ... that I may gain Christ" (Phil. 3:8).

---

[1]Charlotte Elliott, "Just As I Am," in *The Baptist Hymnal* (Nashville: Convention Press, 1991), 307.

Listening Guide

1. Some day our faith will become _____, but until then we must

   learn to _____.

2. Waiting can either _____ us or _____ us, depending
   on our perspective.

3. We must learn to have an _____ perspective.

4. Sometimes we get discouraged because we're not waiting on _____

   but rather we're simply waiting on things _____ God.

Leader Guide

Steps for Leading This Study

Step 1. Begin publicity four weeks before the Introductory Session. Tell whether childcare is provided and if participants will pay for their books.

Step 2. Order books for members and the leader kit which provides DVDs.

Step 3. Reserve a meeting room, a TV, a DVD player, and a CD/tape player.

Step 4. Study *Walking by Faith*; view videos ahead of the group (20-25 mins. each, including music video).

Step 5. Enlist 1) hospitality assistant to greet women, prepare nametags, and plan refreshments;. 2) prayer assistant.

Step 6. Prepare a journal page similar to the one below or download it from www.jenniferroth-schild.com/walking; distribute them in each session.

Walking by Faith Journal

Session _____ Date: _____

Section 1: As I enter this room _____

Section 2: As I enter God's presence _____

Section 3: I bring with me this treasure _____

Section 4: I go out with this treasure _____

Section 5: Lord, hear our prayers _____

Section 6: Lord, hear my prayer _____

Step 7. Bathe your meeting room in prayer. Ask the Holy Spirit to make His presence evident. Praise God for inhabiting His Word and being the living Word. Confess any sins that hamper growth in your faith. Finally, pray for each woman by name and by need.

Getting Ready

1. Confirm arrangements for your meeting room, audiovisual equipment, and childcare.

2. Ask your hospitality assistant to contact everyone registered, affirming their decision to participate.

3. Provide names to your prayer assistant; ask her to join you in praying each week of this study.

Introductory Session

Before the Session

1. Place a three-by-five-inch card on each chair.

2. Provide the journal page on each chair (step 6).

Gathering

1. Greet participants. Distribute nametags and books.

2. Ask each participant to begin looking through her book to find each week's "Textbook Treasures." Ask members to choose one passage that is meaningful to them and write it on the notecard.

Introducing

1. Welcome the group. Introduce yourself.

2. Ask ladies (in small groups) to share where or with whom they've learned the greatest life lessons and one reason they chose this study.

3. Introduce Jennifer. Ask someone to read aloud "About the Author" (p. 4). Tell what her stories and insights have meant to you from your preview of the study. Conclude: We'll identify the darkness that challenges our faith by applying the lessons Jennifer learned in her physical darkness.

4. Encourage participants to journal. Say: Each week, we will begin with "As I Enter This Room," recording things that clamor for our attention (distractions, physical and emotional concerns). This reassures us we won't forget things needing our attention while we participate in this study. (Pause as participants write.) Follow with silent prayer (members may write in "As I enter God's presence"). This will help us focus on our group and enhance our ability to hear from God. (Pause as participants pray.) Briefly thank God for His presence and the gift of faith.

Highlighting

1. Everyone has one "Textbook Treasure" on a card. Challenge them to memorize one each week. Ask participants to record the verse they chose in Journal section 3 and to share why it is meaningful to them.

2. Turn to page 8. Explain: Each week begins with a story from Jennifer illustrating the week's theme, "Textbook Treasures," and "Prepare to Enter the Classroom." The activities insure we don't rush past important truths or miss ways to apply them. Ask participants to set aside 30 minutes each day and to journal thoughts, feelings, and prayers.

3. Answer questions concerning the study or group.

Viewing

1. Each week includes a video featuring Jennifer's teaching, story-telling, and singing. Have members turn to the Listening Guide on page 7.

2. Watch the Introductory Session video.

> ANSWERS: *1. Faith, Sight; 2. soul, circumstance;*
> *3. governed, sight; 4. guide; 5. good, hard, faith, sight*

3. Complete "I go out with this treasure" using the most meaningful challenge, truth, or Scripture.

Blessing

1. Ask for prayer concerns specifically related to starting and finishing this study. Record these in the journal section 5.

2. Replay "It Is Well"; complete journal section 6 with members' individual concerns.

3. When the music ends, thank those attending and wish them God's blessings as they begin week 1.

Session 1: Take a Step

Before the Session

1. Hospitality assistant contacts members and prepares nametags with name and "Take the First Step!"

2. Prepare journal pages and place one on each chair.

3. Post large sheets of paper labeled "Wall of Faith," and provide markers.

Gathering

1. Distribute prepared nametags.

2. Invite members to record the phrases describing their spiritual mentors on the Wall of Faith posters (p. 12).

Introducing

1. Read together this week's Textbook Treasures.

2. Fill in journal sections 1 and 2.

3. Pray for the group session.

Highlighting

1. Ask members to gather definitions of faith from day 1 (p. 10) and share their thoughts from the question on page 22. Add comments to the Wall of Faith.

2. Review the keys to a confident stride from day 2 (remain centered; follow a mental map; listen to the Teacher). Call for responses from page 15. Use this discussion to encourage daily prayer and Bible study.

3. Listen to member responses about God's pursuit, protection, provision, and proof (p. 19). God can be trusted. Encourage members to share personal examples.

4. Share Scriptures from day 5 (p. 24) in groups of three. Lead members to fill in journal section 3.

Viewing

1. View the session 1 video.

> ANSWERS: *1. treasures; 2. treasures, comforts;*
> *3. unexpected; 4. believes, assumes; 5. fear, faith;*
> *6. feeling, awe; 7. highly, lowly*

2. Fill in journal section 4.

3. Discuss fears and feelings from Listening Guide statements 5-7. Share related prayer concerns.

4. Complete journal section 5.

Blessing

1. Replay "Walking by Faith" as members pray, using journal section 6.

2. Ask members to stand; read John 8:12. Instruct pairs to read name tags to each other and swap in order to pray specifically for each other next week.

Session 2: Follow the Leader

Before the Session

1. Have the hospitality assistant contact participants and ask them to bring their Colossians cards.
2. Ask your hospitality assistant to prepare nametags with "Joyful" followed by the person's name.
3. Prepare the journal page.

Gathering

1. Distribute prepared nametags.
2. Direct members to the activity. Ask them to seek out the woman they prayed for last week.

Introducing

1. Distribute the journal page; lead members to fill in sections 1 and 2; pray for the group session.
2. Have pairs share which story of following God's leadership is most like their own—Israel in the desert (day 1) or Peter on the water (day 3).

Highlighting

Use this discussion and the Colossians cards to fill in journal section 3.

Viewing

1. View the session 2 video.

    ANSWERS: *1. control, follow; 2. restfully follow;*

    3. Martyr, Pollyanna, Denier; 4. sufficient, grace

    5. thorns, from, through

2. Fill in journal section 4.

Blessing

1. Read Jeremiah 29:11-13.
2. Record impediments to joy as prayer concerns in journal section 5. Replay "Amazing Grace" as members complete journal section 6.
3. If members have not already done so, ask them to choose an accountability partner. Direct them to set a time to talk and pray together each week.

Session 3: Choose the Right Response

Before the Session

1. Prepare the journal page for this session.
2. Provide a basket, paper strips, pens, and these instructions: Skim the Book of Philippians. Write and place in the basket one phrase that helps you rejoice.

Gathering

Ask your prayer assistant to greet members and record any answers they received to their personal prayer concerns in these first three weeks.

Introducing

1. Distribute the journal page; lead members to fill in journal sections 1 and 2; pray for the session.
2. In pairs, read Psalm 27:5-6 to discover what God does "in the day of trouble" and how the psalmist responded. Choose a situation from page 11; discuss what God has done or will do and your response.

Highlighting

1. Review insights on prayer and on being "pure in heart" from day 1 (p. 45). Ask the question that concludes day 1. Then ask for participants' experiences completing the assignment on page 47.
2. Ask what statements participants most needed from the content. Ask: How did the Scriptures on patience (pp. 52-53) shape your perspective on God's discipline?
3. Complete journal section 3.

Viewing

1. View the session 3 video.

    ANSWERS: *1. difficult gifts; 2. control, response;*

    3. Rejoice, Pray, thanks; 4. initiate, allows

2. Fill in journal section 4.
3. Share responses to the review activity at the end of day 5. Fill in journal section 5.

Blessing

1. Pass the basket until all slips are distributed. Read the phrases aloud.
2. Jennifer said, "When we learn to be truly grateful for His greatest gift, we'll learn to gratefully receive any other gift He may allow" (p. 49). Invite members to complete journal section 6 with this truth in mind.
3. Pray, thanking God for the gift of Jesus.

Session 4: Run with Endurance
Before the Session

1. Ask your prayer assistant to remind participants to complete "Prepare to Enter the Classroom." Encourage her to pray with members for their courage to do so.
2. Prepare this session's journal page.
3. Ask your hospitality assistant to gather large food cans and place blank labels around them.
4. Post the three statements from page 64.

Gathering

Give each participant a can. Instruct them to write three good things in their lives on the blank label. They are to carry the can until instructed otherwise.

Introducing

1. In small groups, share the good things written on the cans. Identify how these good things pull you away from a deeper relationship with God. Now, permit members to "set aside" these weights.
2. Distribute the journal page; use insights from this discussion to complete journal section 1.
3. Read aloud Hebrews 12:1-3 before members fill in journal section 2; pray for the session.

Highlighting

1. Share in small groups the words that best describe members' love for God and their responses to the two questions following (p. 61). Ask, When was the last time you caught a glimpse of Jesus (p. 62)? Let them continue to share.

2. Say, The four pitfalls we studied this week hamper our faith-ability! Assign groups one of four pitfalls; ask them to choose a key sentence from the content and a key Scripture. Hear reports after five minutes.
3. Say, Share one of the posted statements you need to remember. Fill in journal section 3.

Viewing

1. View the session 4 video.
   ANSWERS: *1. universal, escapable; 2. weights, sins; 3. fall, worship, presence, weakness, strength, repentance, purity*
2. Fill in journal section 4.
3. Share responses to the prayer activity concluding day 5. Use these responses to prompt members' prayer requests for the journal page's fifth section.

Blessing

Encourage using the prayer technique in "Prepare to Enter the Classroom" on page 59. Replay "To Be Like You" as members complete journal section 6.

Session 5: Remember God's Word
Before the Session

1. Have five members prepare a short insight from weeks 1-5 and a Scripture to pray back to God.
2. Continue praying with your prayer assistant.
3. Prepare this session's journal page.
4. Post signs for weeks 1-5 in the room.
5. Prepare 10 "times" for practicing the clock strategy of recalling Scripture (p. 84).
6. Provide inexpensive prizes for the gathering activity.

Gathering

1. Have the hospitality assistant ask members for examples of useless memories (such as old addresses).
2. Award prizes for the most creative answers.

Introducing

1. Distribute journal pages; fill in sections 1 and 2; pray for the session.

2. Divide members equally between the 5 stations. Say: Let's remember key insights with the help of (call the women's names). They will review one week's content and pray that week's Scripture back to God. Signal groups to rotate every 90 seconds.

3. Use this information to complete journal section 3.

Highlighting

1. Hear information from day 2, polling people who memorize Scripture and list their strategies.

2. Practice the clock strategy of recalling Scripture; write a "time" on the board; have members recite matching Scriptures. Repeat until all examples are used.

3. Quote C.H. Spurgeon: "Meditation is the best beginning of prayer, and prayer is the best conclusion of meditation" (*www.spurgeon.org*). Ask how Scripture memory and meditation enhance prayer for members. Write this quote in journal section 4.

Viewing

1. View the session 5 video.
   ANSWERS: *1. sight, memory; 2. reflection, truth; 3. weapon, fight; 4. " 'It is written.' "; 5. become*

2. Based on the listening guide, hear members' prayer concerns; fill in journal section 5.

Blessing

1. Take turns reading aloud the scriptural truths of what God says about you (bottom of p. 87).

2. Read aloud the final two paragraphs of day 5; ask members to fill in journal section 6.

Session 6: Wait on God

Before the Session

1. Prepare this session's journal page.

2. Prepare slips of paper with these references from the Book of John: 2:11; 8:49-50,54; 12:23,27-28; 13:31-32; 14:12-13; 16:13-15; 17:1-5,24.

3. Ask your hospitality assistant to arrange refreshments prominently as participants arrive.

Gathering

Have your hospitality assistant greet members; insist that they wait on getting refreshments.

Introducing

1. In small groups, share synonyms for delight (p. 92). Read Psalm 37:4; note the link between delight and desire. Ask if answers reflect God's desires or ours.

2. Distribute journal page; use this discussion to complete sections 1 and 2. Pray sentence prayers expressing members' desires for this final session.

Highlighting

1. Recall answers to the final two activities on page 93.

2. In pairs, review day 3—one focusing on "Tears Cleanse" and the other on "Tears Protect." Hear key insights as a large group.

3. Review the story of Lazarus' death and members' answers to questions related to John 11 (p. 98).

4. Highlight the two paragraphs regarding the glory of God beginning near the bottom of page 98. Assign to pairs the verses from John. Discuss how God's glory makes waiting on God worthwhile.

5. Pause and fill in journal sections 3 and 4.

6. In pairs review the five truths from page 101. Fill in journal section 5 with your request to God on behalf of the church.

Viewing

1. View the session 6 video.
   ANSWERS: *1.) sight, wait; 2.) strengthen, deplete; 3.) eternal; 4.) God, from*

2. Use the Listening Guide's four statements to form a prayer for the journal section 6.

Blessing

1. Replay "Someday." As the song concludes, pray your blessing for the group.

2. Invite everyone to fellowship and have refreshments before saying goodbye.

ENJOY THE BIBLE STUDY?
Experience the music ... again!

**Walking by Faith
The Music Captured Live**

Experience the seven songs you heard during the Bible study, plus three additional songs, including a reprise of the traditional hymn, "It Is Well with My Soul."

ISBN 0-9812-0050-2
Music CD

**Walking by Faith
The Music Videos**

Enjoy the beauty and gracefulness of the music videos from the *Walking by Faith* Bible study. On DVD.

ISBN 0-9812-0050-9
DVD Video

**Along the Way
Songs from the Early Years**

You can hear the most requested songs from two of Jennifer's earlier albums, "Out of the Darkness" and "Come to the Morning." If you enjoyed the music from *Walking by Faith*, you'll treasure the music and lyrics Jennifer wrote "along the way."

ISBN 0-9812-0049-2
Music CD

find these and other products at
WWW.JENNIFERROTHSCHILD.COM

Keep in touch with Jennifer

Jennifer Rothschild • 1730 E Republic Rd., Suite A-220, Springfield, MO 65804 • jr@jenniferrothschild.com • www.jenniferrothschild.cor

BELIEVING IS SEEING!

ISBN 1-59052-047-5

"Lessons I Learned in the Dark is gripping. I don't know the person to whom it has nothing to say."

—BETH MOORE

"Believing is seeing" is one of the most important lessons God has taught Jennifer Rothschild since a retinal disease began claiming her eyesight more than 20 years ago. "This is not a book about blindness," says Jennifer. "It's a book about learning how to really see." With warmth and humor, she shares the guiding principles she walks by and shows you how to:

- Move with freedom, even in confining circumstances.

- Hear echoes of hope, even in heartache.

- Be empowered, even when you don't feel strong.

"At times life is dark for all of us," says the author, "but you can walk forward by faith right into His marvelous light."

Multnomah® Publishers
For a Christian store near you, call 800-991-7747

Keeping Your Trust...One Book at a Time®
www.multnomahbooks.com or www.lifeway.com

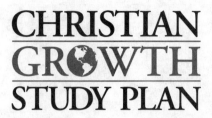

CHRISTIAN GROWTH STUDY PLAN

In the Christian Growth Study Plan (formerly Church Study Course), this book *Walking by Faith: Lessons Learned in the Dark* is a resource for course credit in the subject area Personal Life of the Christian Growth category of plans. To receive credit, read the book, complete the learning activities, show your work to your pastor, a staff member or church leader, then complete the following information. This page may be duplicated. Send the completed page to:

Christian Growth Study Plan
One LifeWay Plaza, Nashville, TN 37234-0117
FAX: (615)251-5067, Email: *cgspnet@lifeway.com*
For information about the Christian Growth Plan, refer to the Christian Growth Study Plan Catalog. It is located online at *www.lifeway.com/cgsp*. If you do not have access to the Internet, contact the Christian Growth Study Plan office (1.800.968.5519) for the specific plan you need for your ministry.

Walking by Faith
Course Number: CG-0846

PARTICIPANT INFORMATION

Social Security Number (USA ONLY-optional)	Personal CGSP Number*	Date of Birth (MONTH, DAY, YEAR)

Name (First, Middle, Last)	Home Phone

Address (Street, Route, or P.O. Box)	City, State, or Province	Zip/Postal Code

Please check appropriate box: ☐ Resource purchased by self ☐ Resource purchased by church ☐ Other

CHURCH INFORMATION

Church Name

Address (Street, Route, or P.O. Box)	City, State, or Province	Zip/Postal Code

CHANGE REQUEST ONLY

☐ Former Name

☐ Former Address	City, State, or Province	Zip/Postal Code

☐ Former Church	City, State, or Province	Zip/Postal Code

Signature of Pastor, Conference Leader, or Other Church Leader	Date

*New participants are requested but not required to give SS# and date of birth. Existing participants, please give CGSP# when using SS# for the first time. Thereafter, only one ID# is required. **Mail to:** Christian Growth Study Plan, One LifeWay Plaza, Nashville, TN 37234-0117. Fax: (615)251-5067.

Rev. 3-03